"We all face adversity, pain, and trials. God calls us — and gives us the strength — to rise above *everything* that comes our way. My friend, Robert Rogers, shares practical and inspirational encouragement that will touch your heart."

Dan Busby, President, ECFA
(Evangelical Council for Financial Accountability)

"When God writes a story not of your own making, you know that the wisdom that arises from that story is profound. Robert's latest book represents the latest gleanings from a life that has experienced trial, persistence, redemption, and joy. For all who have walked through the wilderness, I highly recommend learning from Robert."

William F. High, Chief Executive Officer, NCF
(National Christian Foundation) *Heartland*

"Robert Rogers has suffered unthinkable tragedy in his young life, and has found the presence and love of God in the midst of it all. This little book, his simple, though not easy, "recipe" for surviving whatever suffering life may bring, is an indispensable help for those who seek God when sorrow and pain seem too much to bear."

Bishop Michael Sheridan, Diocese of Colorado Springs

"Few people can match the expertise of Robert Rogers on how to effectively navigate through tragic loss. Having experienced the horrific deaths of his wife and four children, Robert teaches us how he, through the Grace of God, has risen above that despair, and how we can do the same in our lives no matter what circumstances we face."

William Croyle, author of *I Choose to be Happy: A School Shooting Survivor's Triumph over Tragedy*

"My good friend, Robert Rogers, shares Biblical steps that he applies to every trial in order to experience God's restoration. Robert's insightful use of Scriptures and his transparent practical illustrations make this book a must-read for anyone seeking joy amidst suffering."

Mitch Kruse, author and host of *The Restoration Road with Mitch Kruse*

Also by Robert Rogers:

Into the Deep: one man's story of how tragedy took his family but could not take his faith (Tyndale, 2007)

7 Steps to No Regrets: How to find peace of mind with God, others, and yourself (Mighty in the Land Ministry, 2013)

How to Heal the Hurts and Overcome the Worst

Robert Rogers

Mighty in the Land Ministry

Fort Wayne, Indiana

iv

Rise Above
Copyright © 2015 by Robert Rogers
All rights reserved.

Published by *Mighty in the Land Ministry*
Fort Wayne, Indiana 46825
www.MightyInTheLand.com
260-515-5158

Editors: Rosemary Henderson, Kevin Sullivan, & Grace Robinson
Cover design by Hannah Royce, *Helps2*, Fresno, CA.
Author photo by Kevin Ellers.
ISBN-13: 978-0-692-50729-2
Printed in the United States of America
First edition: October 2015

Dedicated to my family,

Inga Elizabeth – my beloved bride,

and our cherished children:

Ezekiel Thomas,

Estellah Eve,

Leo George,

and Lola Elizabeth.

I truly can't fathom how our sovereign God has graced
me with your priceless presence, nor the painful,
sacrosanct journey that brought us to be a family.

Neither can I imagine life without any one of you.

Each of you is precious, honored, loved, and adored
beyond measure – by Almighty God and me.

"And God will wipe away every tear from their eyes; there shall be no more death, nor sorrow, nor crying. There shall be no more pain, for the former things have passed away.
...Behold, I make all things new."

(Revelation 21:4-5 NKJV)

"But those who wait on the LORD will find new strength. They will fly high on wings like eagles. They will run and not grow weary. They will walk and not faint."

(Isaiah 40:31)

Contents

Step 1

Step 2

Step 3

Prologue

What if?

> *"Mr. Rogers, we need to ask you to identify the bodies of your three youngest children. They are dead."*

These piercing words from the officer and chaplain sliced the darkness of my dimly lit hospital room in Emporia, Kansas, early Sunday morning, August 31, 2003. They changed my life forever. No mortal words can ever begin to remotely describe that moment – nor the anguish that followed.

No doubt, you can relate. You've experienced a heartbreak, catastrophe, or excruciating loss that defies explanation. The bottom has fallen out, and you know that life will never again be the same.

Have you found that sometimes, when you hit rock-bottom, when your legs have been knocked out from under you, when you feel as if life can't get any worse, it often does? Why does life simultaneously slam you from the north, south, east, and west – and then once again right in the middle of your gut, just for good measure – often when you are at your weakest and most vulnerable moment?

Wave after wave, it happened to me.

Hours earlier in the darkness on Saturday night, as we returned from a relative's wedding in Wichita, an unfathomable flash-flood inundated our minivan along the Kansas turnpike. It thrust our vehicle off the highway, plunged us into the deluge, and washed half of our precious family out the window while our three youngest children were still strapped in their car seats. After I nearly drowned, tossed by the tumult for over half a mile, somehow I washed ashore and was later brought to a nearby hospital.

There, some eight hours later, after the rescue workers found three of our children, I painfully swallowed the grim and grueling task of identifying our sons, Zachary Seth (5), Nicholas Adam (3), and our newly-adopted daughter from China, Alenah WenYing (1). Hours later, I received word that our oldest daughter, Makenah Alexandra (8), was found in the tempestuous darkness, caught on a barbed-wire fence nearby our overturned automobile – over a mile and a half from the freeway. I had to agonizingly identify her, holding on to hope that somehow my beloved bride of nearly 12 years, Melissa, was still alive. Three dreadful days later on Tuesday morning, my hopes of embracing any of my dear family members again were utterly dashed.

All I cherished most was gone: every dream and every hope.

What was left to live for?

What reason did I have to continue?

Have you been there?

When you're the one traversing the valley of death, every loss is uniquely overwhelming, regardless of the magnitude or circumstances.

What matters most, I've found, is how you respond to the wreckage and remnants of what remains.

Where do you run after the ruin? Where do you hide?

When life devastates you, what inundates you?

"Those who live in the shelter of the Most High will find rest in the shadow of the Almighty." (Psalm 91:1-2)

Where do you run? Where do you dwell? What holds you up?

When I first received the horrifying news of my three youngest children in the Emporia hospital, I slipped my shivering, frail frame out from under the scant bed sheets, braced my feet firmly on the floor, and faced those horrifying words that every parent dreads.

I had to face it. I couldn't escape. I couldn't hide from the horror.

"Where could I go to escape from you? Where could I get away from your presence?" (Psalm 139:7 GNT)

Where else could I run but back to God's embrace?

"Lord, to whom would we go? You alone have the words that give eternal life. We believe them, and we know you are the Holy One of God." (John 6:68-69)

Somehow, by the grace of God, I gripped the pain and faced my fears head-on: death, utter loss, uncertain future, and other qualms. I wasn't about to give up, but I felt as though my faith was about to give in.

It felt as if God clasped the back of my head, shoved my face deep into the demise, and said in essence, "Go ahead, Robert. Face it. My Son, Jesus, died on the cross. He knows. He will give you the strength you need. My grace really is *that* sufficient, beloved child of mine."

"My grace is all you need, for my power is greatest when you are weak." (2 Corinthians 12:9 GNT)

I first had to give God permission. I had to allow Him in – when it hurt the most – and when trusting Him once again seemed the most difficult. I had to open the painful door of my heart to Him once again. *"Here I stand at the door and knock. If you hear me calling and open the door, I will come in, and we will share a meal as friends."* (Revelation 3:20)

We each have that choice when life slams us into the side of a mountain. We can slam the door in God's face, bolt it, and lock it. We can defy God and turn our backs on Him when life turns on us. Conversely, we can run to God's arms and allow Him Who holds our healing to hold our hearts as we grieve.

Amidst the feebleness from my greatest fears emerged a manifestation of God's greatest might.

It involves enormous faith, fortitude, and prayer. It requires steadfast relationship with God through a personal encounter with His Son, Jesus Christ. It demands active, living faith, for *"faith without actions is dead."* (James 2:26 GNT)

Before God *"allowed me to suffer much hardship"* (Psalm 71:20), everything must first have been filtered through His mighty fingers, as in Job's life. (Job 1:12 and 2:6) Job lost his health, his business, and all ten of his children. Yet, without question, God ultimately *"will restore me to life again and lift me up from the depths of the earth."* (Psalm 71:20) Indeed, He *"will restore me to even greater honor and comfort me once again."* (Psalm 71:21) God did it for Job. He did it for His beloved Son, Jesus. He will do it for you.

Even if we know these scriptures and our faith remains somehow intact, our souls often remain messed up and wounded. Thank God, my faith still believed. Still, my soul needed surgery and rehabilitation.

Yes, I believe that God *"restores my soul."* (Psalm 23:3 NIV) But, how can He? How will He?

How?

"I do believe, but help me overcome my unbelief!" (Mark 9:24)

How can God take a wretch like me, a mess like mine, and restore it to anything worthwhile? Looking at the circumstances and carnage, it seems absolutely impossible and unfathomable, doesn't it? Yet, God's ways are not our ways. *"For just as the heavens are higher than the earth, so my ways are higher than your ways and my thoughts higher than your thoughts."* (Isaiah 55:9)

Scripture encourages us not to *"look at the troubles we can see now; rather, we fix our gaze on things that cannot be seen. For the things we see now will soon be gone, but the things we cannot see will last forever."* (2 Corinthians 4:18)

It is a process, for certain. It takes time. It takes tears. Weeping is good. I found that tears help to wash away tiny specs of grief, one at a time. They hurt, yes, but they heal. Tears are vital to our very existence and recovery.

Now, years later, out of absolute obedience to God's call, and by invitation alone, I still freely share His Good News through our family's story, travelling the country and parts of the world. Certainly, people are struck by the catastrophe that overtook my family. However, further in, people want to know "how" I made it. How do I still navigate through the unrelenting pain of the past, particularly as I recount raw emotions from my heart hundreds upon hundreds of times to all who invite me?

"How" is one of the most often asked questions of me during the first decade after the flash-flood that ushered my dear family Home. "How do you cope?" "How did you make it through?"

People want and need to know. "How can I get through my trauma?" "How can I navigate these excruciating and overpowering waters?" The short answer is, "Only God."

As the police in Kansas and later in Missouri requested me to deliver two local press conferences, hopeful words emerged from deep within me, all by the sheer grace of our sovereign God.

"We will get through this. We will rise above this. And by God's grace, good will somehow come from this." (Emporia, Kansas – Press Conference, September 1, 2003)

"When God is our refuge, even when there is despair – there is hope! Even in the midst of sorrow – there is peace and joy! This tragedy may have shattered my family, but it will not shatter my resolve to hope for good. I'm fully persuaded that somehow, by His grace, He will turn this tragedy into good." (Liberty, Missouri – Press Conference, September 3, 2003)

Through this book, in a very straightforward and practical way, I'll strive to answer *how* God can heal *your* hurts. I'll offer three simple steps to assist you on your road to recovery. They are simple, yes, but not easy. If you can traverse these three steps, you'll be on the right trajectory to rise up from the waters beyond your adversity and soar with the eagles.

"But those who trust in the Lord for help will find their strength renewed. They will rise on wings like eagles; they will run and not get weary; they will walk and not grow weak." (Isaiah 40:31 GNT)

If your world is suddenly washed away or turned upside-down, I sincerely want you to be able to *Rise Above* your circumstance and situation. Please consider these words and take them to heart. It has literally cost me everything to share them with you. I pray they take root and dramatically transform your life.

Step 1
Chapter One

You Choose

> *"Today I have given you the choice between life and death, between blessings and curses. Now I call on heaven and earth to witness the choice you make. Oh, that you would choose life, so that you and your descendants might live!"*   (Deuteronomy 30:19)

Life has always been a choice. Since the dawn of time on earth, Adam and Eve faced a choice. Still to this day, we have the choice to obey God or follow the devil's deceptions. We face choices every day for good or evil, for blessings or curses.

To *Rise Above* your situation, first choose to overcome the adversity. Rather than remain comfortable and complacent in your conundrum, crave something better – something that surpasses your sadness. Decide that you will no longer remain a victim, but that someway, somehow, you are going to get through this and emerge victorious.

Resolve right now in your heart, mind, and attitude that God is about to use your set-back as a set-up for God to show up and show off! God can display His glory through your predicament – if you will let Him. As a wise man instructed me soon after the flash-flood, "Robert, out of every great test can emerge a great testimony."

To *Rise Above*, you have to choose life; not merely sustaining, survival mentality, or just-getting-by day-by-day. Rather, believe that you can still live a truly vibrant, abundant life the way God intended. *"I have come that they may have life, and have it to the full."* (John 10:10 NIV)

Joy and misery are both choices. Just as no one can make you happy, neither can anyone make you miserable. It's up to you. Choose life. Choose joy.

I was determined not to remain dejected, downhearted, or despondent, but rather to seek out and unearth the good that only God could bring forth. I was determined to remain thankful amidst what felt like an apparent betrayal and breach of my faith by God.

How did this flash-flood happen? Why? Why did God allow this? Why didn't God prevent it or protect our family, despite our steadfast faith and persistent prayers for travel safety?

I don't know. I may never know the answers this side of Heaven. Yet, if I trust God implicitly, I don't have to know. I can still have peace, regardless. Trying to figure out God, or beating my head against a wall attempting to make sense of it all is simply not worth it. I had to accept it. In the words of T.S. Eliot, "The only way to alter the past is to accept it."

The past is past. No one can change it. Accept it.

Accept what happened, whether or not it was your fault. Perhaps you made a personal choice that partially caused it. Okay. Accept it, own it, and take responsibility to remedy it as best you can. Perhaps something happened to you beyond your control, and now you are left to pick up the pieces. The divorce papers just arrived, the fire demolished your home, you just miscarried your baby, the economy wrecked your business, the doctor delivered the diagnosis, the storm consumed your family, or the catastrophe demolished your dream. Denying it won't make it any better. Accepting reality can help to mend it.

As Apostle Paul aptly suggested, *"You must accept whatever situation the Lord has put you in."* (1 Corinthians 7:17) Accept that somehow, regardless of how confounded and unexplainable, God has placed you right where you are – in the middle of this painful predicament. For some greater purpose in His omnipotent sovereignty, He would rather you traverse through this valley than extract you out of its clutches. Even though horrible suffering and agonizing death awaited Jesus, when the time came, *"He steadfastly set His face to go to Jerusalem."* (Luke 9:51 NKJV) Jesus accepted it and *"made up his mind."* (Luke 9:51 GNT)

Accept it and begin the healing process right away. To delay further will only prolong the agony, compound the bitterness, and suspend the remedy.

Don't ignore it. Don't live in denial for the rest of your life. You'll only postpone indefinitely the fabulous future that God has hand-crafted for you.

1st Step to Rise Above: *Face It*.

Yes, *Face It*. Admit it. Accept it. Don't deny reality. Don't pretend it never happened. Don't ignore it or try to brush it under the rug. Don't avoid going to the cemetery. Don't keep that skeleton hidden in the closet. Acknowledge reality. At the same time, step out in faith and declare God's reality from His Holy Word. Rather than tell God how big your problem is, tell your problem how big God is.

I realize this can be terribly difficult. It sounds simple, but it's not easy. Boldly confront the dreadful situation head-on, just as I tearfully faced my children's precious, yet lifeless bodies within hours of their deaths. Every loss can be acutely devastating. This was, undoubtedly, a humanly impossible undertaking. Apart from the gracious strength of Almighty God, there was no way I was utterly able. For this very reason, a continual and personal relationship with Him is vitally essential. I never could have faced it if I hadn't first known God personally through Jesus Christ. No way. *"God is our refuge and strength, always ready to help in times of trouble."* (Psalm 46:1)

To choose life means to surrender the past. For a revival to come forth, a death must often occur first, just as the birth of spring follows the death of winter. *"I tell you the truth, unless a kernel of wheat is planted in the soil and dies, it remains alone. But its death will produce many new kernels — a plentiful harvest of new lives."* (John 12:24) Through your agonizing death, God can bring forth abundant life.

This can seem daunting at first, I admit. The last thing I wanted to do was let go of my family and our dreams for a long life together. I wasn't ready. It was too soon. I didn't want to let that part of me die. I wanted to hold on. This tragedy happened much too suddenly and abruptly.

Yet, I had no other choice.

Either I was doomed to wallow in my mire for the rest of my earthly life, or I would choose to wade through the waters to find a way out. For *"at the time you are put to the test, he will give you the strength to endure it, and so provide you with a way out."* (1 Corinthians 10:13 GNT)

I found that it required an attitude adjustment on my part, to adopt the outlook of Christ, *"for we have the mind of Christ."* (1 Corinthians 2:16) I've heard it said that "attitude is everything" and "attitude determines your altitude." I believe both are true. The attitude you choose will determine the altitude to which you'll rise.

To acquire a Christ-like attitude requires me to know His nature, and to know Him personally through relationship. It first involves a choice to accept Him as my Lord, and then to develop a deeper relationship through time and daily discipline. As I abandon myself, I become more like Jesus. Just as Noah built the ark, I also need to fortify the ark of my faith, fostering it daily through a deepening relationship with God and His Word.

If you'll do this, I confidently believe that you will *Rise Above* your adversity.

You will overcome your obstacle.

You will persevere through the pressure.

You will triumph over the tragedy.

You will emerge better, not bitter.

You will cultivate your character.

You will fortify your faith.

You will have to make a concerted effort to choose all these things. Choose your attitude. It may cause some additional pain to *Face It*. The pain of that decision may weigh a few ounces. However, the pain of regrets weighs tons. If you don't *Face It* now, you will likely regret it exponentially and immensely more forever. The longer you wait, the more daunting the difficulty becomes. As I've ministered and shared my story hundreds upon hundreds of times, I've encountered people who are still "stuck in a rut" of pain, sinking deeper into the quicksand of despair, all because they never fully faced it.

As you well know, we are not in Heaven yet. So, life and people are implicitly full of problems. Life is not fair, but God is still good. Death is not fair. Divorce, cancer, disease, disabilities, miscarriages, prejudices, injustices, layoffs, hurricanes, tornados, floods, disasters, traffic jams, interruptions, and even detours are not fair. We are not promised a life that is easy or fair. *"Here on earth you will have many trials and sorrows. But take heart, because I have overcome the world."* (John 16:33)

God wants to release you from the pain and power of your past. So, *"let all who are discouraged take heart."* (Psalm 34:2) Choose life. Take heart. Choose to *Face It*.

Something remarkable happens. The fear, worry, and dread will gradually begin to diminish. What you inevitably face may be fearful, indeed. Don't shy or cower away. Charge at it head-on like a bull. Don't be controlled by it. As you take courage to *Face It*, you also begin to defuse it.

After the birth of my son, Zachary, two unfamiliar words of enormous implication – "Down syndrome" –

were daunting at first. The first inclination of my flesh was to flinch away. However, I faced the diagnosis and didn't ignore it. I gripped the uncertainty with all my might. I found that fear quickly dissipated as love for my son dominated, for *"perfect love drives out fear."* (1 John 4:18 NIV)

As a brave, young boy, King David faced the fear of the giant, Goliath. Gripped by fear, none in the Israelite army had enough courage or faith to confront Goliath and the Philistines. Left unchecked, fear can paralyze even an entire nation. Yet, wiry, scrawny David faced him. In fact, he charged towards everyone's greatest fear. *"As Goliath moved closer to attack, David quickly ran out to meet him."* (1 Samuel 17:48) Run towards that which you fear.

Many years later, King David had to face an entirely different kind of fear: that of sin, shame, and consequences. He had committed adultery with Bathsheba and arranged the death of her husband. Then, Nathan, the prophet brought David face to face with his fear through his convicting words, *"You are that man!"* (2 Samuel 12:7)

Jonah tried to dodge his fear of the people of Nineveh when he boarded a ship to avert God and them. *"But Jonah got up and went in the opposite direction to get away from the LORD. He bought a ticket and went on board, hoping to escape from the LORD by sailing to Tarshish."* (Jonah 1:3) Fear controlled Jonah until he faced it. Not only that, it nearly brought calamity upon those around him, endangering everyone else on the ship as the storm pummeled them – until he fessed up and faced it.

Job immediately faced the deaths of his ten children, as well as the loss of his business, including numerous servants and some 11,000 head of livestock. *"What I always feared has happened to me. What I dreaded has come true."* (Job 3:25) He exemplified a prime example of how to confront grief and tragedy. *Face It* head-on. Don't try to deny it. Grieve. Lament. Mourn. Cry. Vent. Scream, if necessary. Get it out.

Above all, don't blame God. Instead, worship and thank God. This reaction is counterintuitive and countercultural, but it is the only response that truly works.

"Job stood up and tore his robe in grief. Then he shaved his head and fell to the ground before God. He said, 'I came naked from my mother's womb, and I will be stripped of everything when I die. The LORD gave me everything I had, and the LORD has taken it away. Praise the name of the LORD!' In all of this, Job did not sin by blaming God." (Job 1:20-22)

Job's positive response continues to inspire and challenge us – thousands of years later.

When we refuse to face and deal with issues, then negative consequences – from our actions or inactions – can hurt even those around us, in ways we might never fathom. Conversely, when we choose to face a situation and tackle it with God's grace, then we give Him liberty to work through our mess and bring forth divine mercy and healing amidst it all.

The greatest Good the world has ever known came to fruition only after Mary courageously faced the angel Gabriel and his message, as she responded, *"I am the Lord's servant, and I am willing to accept whatever he wants. May everything you have said come true."* (Luke 1:38) Her "yes" came after she was initially *"confused and disturbed"* (Luke 1:29) and even somewhat *"frightened."* (Luke 1:30) What a supreme example of faith the Blessed Mother gives each of us to face a seemingly impossible circumstance and surrender our will to God's way. Most likely, the greater the impossibility, the greater the glory God has in store. As Mary gave birth to Jesus, we must first *Face It* in order to bring life to God's promise.

God brought glory to His Son, Jesus, as He faced the crucifixion and the cross, even after pleading, *"Father, if you are willing, please take this cup of suffering away from me."* (Luke 22:42) The Holy Spirit supernaturally comforted me while I faced my family's deaths and tearfully muttered, "Lord, into your Hands I commend their spirits" as I identified each one in the hospital ER in Emporia, Kansas.

By facing it through my act of surrender, God began healing my heart and slowly restoring my soul. Consequently, many others drew closer to God as they witnessed His virtue working through me. If I had refused to *Face It*, then God's manifest power might never have been visible to help inspire others.

Apostle Paul had lived a life of terrible regrets. *"I was so zealous that I harshly persecuted the church."* (Philippians 3:6) God completely transformed his life, and Paul faced the regretful wrongs he had committed, preaching the Gospel everywhere.

Facing the difficult past requires great fortitude and courage, whether what happened was your fault or not. Perhaps your personal choices caused it, as King David sinned with Bathsheba (2 Samuel 11), or as Peter denied Jesus three times. (Luke 22:54-62)

Perhaps some uncontrollable outside force caused your situation, such as abuse, divorce, death, or natural disasters. Now you are left to deal with what remains. Regardless, break the power of the past. Don't let it maintain control over you. Take courage. Start trudging through the mess and *Face It*. Begin by taking one step forward, as difficult as it may be.

Chapter Two

Step by Step

"He has watched your every step through this great
wilderness."   (Deuteronomy 2:7)

As I warily approached and entered the Emporia
ER on that horrific night in 2003, I took one step, followed
by another. I kissed death. With much trepidation and
tears, I identified our four children, my very own flesh and
blood. Three days later, I identified my bride's lifeless
body, after eleven years of vibrant, blissful marriage, "till
death do we part." The next day, back in Liberty, Missouri,
I took one step at a time that first morning at home and
each thereafter, waking up and getting out of bed – alone.
That November, I baked a birthday cake for what would
have been our first birthday celebration with Alenah. I
faced Christmas alone in my home, and then New Year's
Eve, when Melissa and I would have celebrated twelve
years of marriage.

Each step along the way was painfully excruciating and yet healing. They were necessary to enable me to eventually *Rise Above*. *"Humanly speaking, it is impossible. But not with God. Everything is possible with God."* (Mark 10:27)

Run towards your pain and *Face It*. Don't avoid or suppress it. Consider asking yourself, "What am I supposed to learn from this challenge?" Realize that a problem is not always a bad thing. Growth only comes through pain. God has designed and custom fit your pain to fortify your faith, patience, endurance, and character. If you attempt to avoid or escape your pain, you'll avoid the gain. You'll miss the enrichment, development, and blessing God has in store. Trust God's sovereign, yet baffling Hand. *"I create the light and make the darkness. I send good times and bad times. I, the LORD, am the one who does these things."* (Isaiah 45:7)

Back in December of 2006, I was headed to the Denver airport in a terrible snow storm. Having left a few hours early that morning, I breathed a sigh of relief after returning the rental car safely and intact. I sped into the terminal with plans to speedily zip home on a flight to Indianapolis. To my dismay, my rapid pace came to a screeching halt. Thousands of people had swamped the ticketing area and backed up the queue lines as the flight monitors displayed nothing but, "Cancelled, Cancelled, Cancelled."

Once I caught my breath and assessed the grim situation, I was able to observe the remarkable behaviors of how people reacted. Irate business travelers pounded the ticket counters, apparently expecting the agent to somehow sprout wings and fly them home. Frantic parents panicked, not knowing if they had enough food, formula, or diapers for their children. Worried holiday travelers became wrecked with anxiety, wondering whether they'd be home for Christmas. We all had to face the fact together that over five thousand of us were stranded in the Denver Airport! We had no choice but to ride out one whale of a blizzard with no end in sight.

Even though we are naturally still shocked by events such as this and news around us, we shouldn't be surprised. *"Here on earth you will have many trials and sorrows."* (John 16:33)

Until we get to Heaven, life on this earth will rarely be smooth and easy, peaches and cream, or peanut butter and jelly. It's a constant journey of breaking and growing, falling and rising, crying and climbing, debilitating and developing. I found it helps "soften the blow" somewhat to simply *Face It* and accept it.

After the flash-flood, and throughout professional grief counseling, I intentionally didn't request any medication. (None was prescribed, either.) I felt as though I needed to feel and experience the raw pain firsthand in order to process and work through it. I needed to *Face It*, rather than escape it. For me, I believe medication would have only suppressed my symptoms. (Everyone is wired differently, and every situation is unique. We all grieve as differently as we all look. Proceed at your own pace. If your physician or therapist prescribes medication for depression or a biochemical condition, it's likely best to heed their advice and follow their treatment regimen.)

Whatever difficulty you're facing, don't suppress it. Get it out constructively, not destructively. Perhaps you might try to journal, paint, walk, run, exercise, compose, play an instrument, dance, build, or even chop wood (which I personally enjoy). For me, walking, exercising, playing the piano, composing lyrics and music, and journaling all helped tremendously to scrape out the inside of my heart and bring it out into the open daylight.

At one point, I strapped my pup-tent and sleeping bag to the back of my bicycle, packed some trail mix, and biked nearly sixty miles on the Katy Trail State Park across Missouri. I camped overnight along the way and rode back the next day. Pumping the bike pedals helped clear my head, purge some tears, and give me perspective, constructively. The rhythm of riding along the rails-to-trails pathway helped me find a new rhythm to the path of my life. Another time I hopped onboard an Amtrak in Kansas City and took a train trip to help process everything. I even went on personal prayer retreats at places like the Abbey of Gethsemani monastery in Kentucky and the Billy

Graham Training Center at The Cove in North Carolina. These moments away helped immensely to heal my heart.

The process of peeling back each layer of the onion, one at a time, will undoubtedly bring tears. However, it is a necessary progression to journey towards your core. Even Jesus needed moments of seclusion and time away, particularly after the horrid beheading of his cousin, John the Baptizer. *"As soon as Jesus heard the news, he left in a boat to a remote area to be alone."* (Matthew 14:13) Cry, grieve, vent, and cleanse your soul in every beneficial way possible. Don't explode like a pressure cooker.

Forgive. A significant part of facing it may involve forgiveness. You'll never *Rise Above* unless you first forgive. Un-forgiveness, in particular, binds God's healing Hands. *"But if you refuse to forgive others, your Father will not forgive your sins."* (Matthew 6:15)

Un-forgiveness can fester and rot away your soul like internal cancer. Let go of that grudge. Don't allow it to decay any longer. Deal with it today. Call or go see that person right now and ask forgiveness. Life is too short, and eternity is too long. What if today were your last heartbeat or their last day? Live a life of no regrets. *"Go and be reconciled to that person. Come to terms quickly with your enemy before it is too late."* (Matthew 5:24-25)

Purge every ounce of that cancerous venom, whether it's a misunderstanding, a miscommunication, a grudge, un-forgiveness, or even betrayal. Purging doesn't entail forgetting, but rather forgiving and cleansing.

"Get rid of all bitterness, passion, and anger. No more shouting or insults, no more hateful feelings of any sort. Instead, be kind and tender-hearted to one another, and forgive one another, as God has forgiven you through Christ." (Ephesians 4:31-32 GNT)

When you don't forgive, you aren't free. You can't begin to *Rise Above.* The person who offended or injured you anchors your spirit to the soil, like a grounded hot air balloon. Perhaps without realizing it, you're empowering them to maintain control over you. You've surrendered power over to them.

When you forgive, it cuts loose the sand bags holding down your balloon and relinquishes that person's influence over your life. Forgiveness doesn't just take the heat off them. It takes the heat off you! Forgiveness restores your freedom to fly and your liberty to live.

The longer you hold onto the offense, the longer that person holds onto you. If you need to forgive, but have difficulty doing so, perhaps try this.

Kneel humbly before God, breathe in deeply three times, and as you exhale each time, say, "I forgive you. Please forgive me. I surrender all."

Breathe out the bitterness, and breathe in the forgiveness. Breathe in Jesus. Sometimes the best way to heal a wound is to expose it. Forgiving may hurt a bit at first. It may cause you to bleed somewhat. That's okay. As it is true throughout the Old and New Testaments, *"Without the shedding of blood, there is no forgiveness of sins."* (Hebrews 9:22) Start the healing process. Begin anew.

Jesus put the utmost premium on forgiving. He emphasized that we *"can pray for anything… But when you are praying, first forgive anyone you are holding a grudge against…"* (Mark 11:24-25) On Calvary, *"…they crucified Jesus there… Jesus said, 'Forgive them, Father! They don't know what they are doing.'"* (Luke 23:33-34 GNT) If He can forgive while being nailed to the cross, then surely Christ can grant you the grace to forgive others who have "nailed" you, if you simply ask Him.

When you are full of bitterness, you are held captive by anger and resentment. If you hold it in, it will hold you back. When life shakes you, similar to a cup brimming full of hot water, it's eventually going to spill out and burn. Bitterness can scald you, and even those you love. Forgiveness, on the other hand, fosters healing.

If you face your challenge, you will face the grace from God to handle it. I firmly believe God will never allow you to endure such severe trauma if He won't also equip and enable you to overcome it. If you will *Face It*, God will grace it. Either you carry your cross, or you will be crushed under the weight of it. I believe it's no accident that Joseph and Jesus were both carpenters. Jesus' cross fit perfectly. Likewise, the cross He hand-crafted for you has a snug fit, divinely designed for you to carry. *"For my yoke is easy to bear, and the burden I give you is light."* (Matthew 11:30) The choice to carry it is yours.

If you don't *Face It*, the problem won't get any better on its own. It won't fade away. You'll likely only drag down others around you in the process, and miss out on the blessings that God has in store on the other side of your brokenness.

When you *Face It* with God's grace, you can confront the issue with the assurance of *"God's peace, which is far more wonderful than the human mind can understand. His peace will guard your hearts and minds as you live in Christ Jesus."* (Philippians 4:7) Then, the sheer testimony of your uplifting attitude through the adversity will impact those watching you navigate this hardship. People are constantly watching to see how you respond. For better or worse, you are witnessing to those around you all the time, simply by the way you react.

As you rely completely on God to pull you through, your personal relationship with Him will delve to a much deeper degree of intimacy than you ever thought possible. You will discover a deeper dimension of God's redemption and restoration as He uses your suffering to refine, realign, reshape, remake, compel, and propel you to a higher level of effectiveness and fruitfulness for Him.

Don't waste your suffering. It is a gift, wrapped in the disguise of demise. Open it. *Face It.*

For nearly three years, I lived alone in my empty, hollow home near Kansas City as I faced all the memories, belongings, clothing, toys, artwork, and mementos of my Heavenly family. It was the worst of times, yet the best of times, as I collapsed constantly into the lap of God and let Him hold me. I literally sensed His Presence as I cried, prayed, and basked in His sacred Scripture. It deepened my knowledge and love of Him dramatically as I shared in *"the fellowship of His sufferings."* (Philippians 3:10 NKJV)

As challenging as it sounds, try to move from asking "Why me?" to "Why not me?" I appreciate how difficult this can be. It took me a long time to shift these gears – from inward wallowing to outward thinking. Consider that perhaps God loves you, trusts you, and thinks so highly of you, that He desires you to endure this obstacle to grow. *"These trials are only to test your faith, to show that it is strong and pure. It is being tested as fire tests and purifies gold – and your faith is far more precious to God than mere gold."* (1 Peter 1:7)

Realize that life is still worth living, despite the anguish you are enduring. This uncommon mindset may require an attitude adjustment. Let it penetrate down to your heart. *"For as he thinks in his heart, so is he."* (Proverbs 23:7 NKJV)

Your attitude will indeed determine your altitude. About five percent of life is *what* happens to you. *How* you respond makes up the other ninety-five percent. Your response is the key. It's not so much what happens *to* you, but what happens *in* you that matters.

Most importantly while you navigate through each dark or difficult turn, don't stay stuck in *"the dark valley of death."* (Psalm 23:4) Don't simply stay put. Instead, *"walk through the dark valley"* (Psalm 23:4) and *"fear no evil"* (Psalm 23:4 NIV) for God is with you.

Keep walking, keep trusting, keep loving, keep serving, keep praying, keep giving, keep thanking, and keep moving. You may not feel like it and there may be no rational reason to keep living. Do it anyway. I can empathize. Don't give up. Don't stop. Keep moving.

I'm convinced that God wants to refine your faith, cultivate your character, and fill you with real hope. He wants the roots of your faith to deepen and strengthen. He wants you to grow, flourish, and bring glory to Him. So, don't simply "get by" and get through it. Rather, go through it – full-throttle and all the way. As you go through it, be sure to grow from it. *"Whenever trouble comes your way, let it be an opportunity for joy. For when your faith is tested, your endurance has a chance to grow. So let it grow, for when your endurance is fully developed, you will be strong in character and ready for anything.*" (James 1:2-4)

Are you truly ready for anything? Buckle up for Step 2.

"Be strong! We are not here to play, to dream, to drift. We have hard work to do and loads to lift. Shun not the struggle. **Face it.** *'Tis God's gift. Be strong!"* (Maltbie D. Babcock – composer of *"This Is My Father's World"* hymn – 1901)

Step 2

Chapter Three

Dive In

> *"Consider it pure joy, my brothers, whenever you face trials of many kinds."* (James 1:2 NIV)

Joseph was dealt a raw deal. As the youngest brother with a loving father, and despite a coat of many colors and prophetic childhood dreams, his life turned for the worse. None of it was fair. His jealous brothers threw him into a pit. He was sold as a slave, taken to Egypt, wrongfully accused, and spent well over a decade in prison.

How many of us would have still considered *"it pure joy"* (James 1:2 NIV) and had a good attitude after all of that? Yet, Joseph continued to follow God faithfully and with impeccable, exemplary character. He faced the hand he was dealt head-on, without flinching. No doubt, he had unanswered questions and emotions. Yet, his faith in God's sovereign providence remained intact.

He didn't stop there.

He dove deeper to the next step.

Are you ready, too? This may be a bit painful.

2nd Step to Rise Above: ***Embrace It.***

Yes. Embrace your hardship. Dive in, head first.

"No! I don't want to embrace this pain!"

You're right. None of us do. That is our first natural response. Even Jesus, *"who for the joy set before him endured the cross"* (Hebrews 12:2 NIV) also *"offered prayers and pleadings, with a loud cry and tears, to the one who could deliver him out of death."* (Hebrews 5:7) He pleaded with His Father, *"Please take this cup of suffering away from me. Yet I want your will, not mine."* (Luke 22:42) Jesus surrendered to the cross to which His Father had appointed Him. He embraced it.

So should we.

"Christ suffered for you. He left you an example. He expects you to follow in his steps. You too were chosen to suffer." (1 Peter 2:21 NIrV) Jesus suffered greatly. As His followers, we shouldn't be surprised when we suffer greatly as well. *"He put up with attacks from sinners. So think about him. Then you won't get tired. You won't lose hope."* (Hebrews 12:3 NIrV)

Until we get to Heaven, pain is a part of life on earth. So, *Embrace It* enthusiastically, and *"don't be surprised at the fiery trials you are going through, as if something strange were happening to you. Instead, be very glad — because these trials will make you partners with Christ in his suffering."* (1 Peter 4:12-13)

I realize it contradicts every fiber of natural inclination, but try it anyway. Rejoice in your trial. Count your suffering as pure joy. Thank God optimistically for your circumstance. *"Always give thanks to God the Father for everything."* (Ephesians 5:20 NIrV) Actively embrace your adversity positively, as you would a Christmas present. It truly is a gift, custom fit by God for your good. *"The suffering you sent was good for me, for it taught me to pay attention to your principles."* (Psalm 119:71)

As frightful and intimidating as your circumstance may appear, realize that God is with you through it all, and He will not permit you to be stretched beyond your breaking point. *"But God keeps his promise, and he will not allow you to be tested beyond your power to remain firm; at the time you are put to the test, he will give you the strength to endure it, and so provide you with a way out."* (1 Corinthians 10:13 GNT) God will indeed make a way where there seems to be no way.

In the profound words of Saint Augustine, "Do you wish to rise? Begin by descending."

In order to *Rise Above*, you must first descend below and utterly *Embrace It*. *"Even when I walk through the dark valley of death, I will not be afraid, for you are close beside me."* (Psalm 23:4) God may be leading you to step down first into the valley before you step up onto the mountaintop.

"He guides me along right paths, bringing honor to his name." (Psalm 23:3)   Even though those paths can seem treacherous and rocky, they are still *"right"* in God's sight. After all, growth takes place in the valleys. It is where we are made, and where we discover of what we are made. Character and faith are forged in the fiery furnace called suffering. Just as muscles don't strengthen from laziness and lethargy, so our faith is fortified by exercising it diligently as we embrace the daily struggles of everyday life.

Although these confounded paths can often seem thorny and rocky, trust God absolutely that His ways are indeed right. *"If you are walking in darkness, without a ray of light, trust in the LORD and rely on your God."* (Isaiah 50:10) He has you right where He wants you, for the greater good and for His greater glory and honor. You may never fully understand or make sense of it, this side of Heaven. *"Now we see things imperfectly, like puzzling reflections in a mirror, but then we will see everything with perfect clarity. All that I know now is partial and incomplete, but then I will know everything completely, just as God now knows me completely."* (1 Corinthians 13:12) We don't see the full picture now. If we could, we probably wouldn't like it or couldn't handle it! Trust God to reveal just enough to illuminate your next step.

"You must accept whatever situation the Lord has put you in, and continue on…" (1 Corinthians 7:17) Who put you smack dab in the middle of your conundrum? The Lord! So, accept it and *Embrace It*. However, don't just remain there. Don't stay stuck in your scars or paralyzed by your

pain. You'll remain ineffective for God. If God brought you to it, He will bring you through it. Don't stay put in the valley. Keep walking, keep trusting, keep thanking, and keep moving. *"Continue on."* Keep stirring the pot. As one of my graduate professors used to say, "It's hard to steer a parked car." In other words, keep your vehicle – your life – moving forward. Then at least God has a chance to guide you in the right direction. If you remain immobilized, God can't very well direct your paths.

As Elijah once fled in fear for his life, *"he went on alone into the wilderness, traveling all day. He sat down under a solitary broom tree and prayed that he might die. 'I have had enough, LORD,' he said. 'Take my life.'"* (1 Kings 19:4) How often do we feel the same as Elijah? We're at the end of our rope. We've had enough, and just want to go Home to be with God. In this moment, Elijah was nearly suicidal. Yet, God had other plans for his life and wilderness journey. *"Then he lay down and slept under the broom tree. But as he was sleeping, an angel touched him and told him, 'Get up and eat!'"* (1 Kings 19:5) Sometimes, God simply wants us to get up and get moving. Even after they *"stoned Paul and dragged him out of town, thinking he was dead…he got up and went back into the town."* (Acts 14:19-20)

Just taking that first step can be the most difficult. After my family died, finding the fortitude and purpose to plant my feet on the floor every morning to begin each day was enormously challenging. Growing up, my father often reminded and motivated me with these words: "Getting started is half done." If I can just get started, I'm already half-way there.

Even now, this same principle helps guide me. I regularly confront the challenge to exercise every day on an elliptical or stationary bike. I rarely ever feel like starting. However, I find that if I can just begin pumping those blasted pedals, then I can fully commit myself for at least 30 minutes. For me, the first step is always the hardest. The same is true with embracing it.

Similarly, when Moses led the Israelites out of Egypt, they appeared trapped in the desert with their backs against the Red Sea. Pharaoh's army, with over 600 of their best chariots, closed in on the Israelites' camp. They complained to Moses, *"Why did you bring us out here to die in the wilderness? Weren't there enough graves for us in Egypt?"* (Exodus 14:11) We're not much different now, are we? Complaining is so easy when times are tough. We don't want to move from our misery. We often look back and wish for the "good-old days," striving to recapture the past. I've come to realize that you can never get back or repeat the past, regardless of how much you might want to do so. We have to embrace the situation at hand and plow through it.

Rather than stay stuck in their tracks, crying and complaining, God urged the Israelites to move onward and take a step of faith. *"Then the LORD said to Moses, 'Why are you crying out to me? Tell the people to get moving!'"* (Exodus 14:15) Just as an automatic sliding door at the grocery store only opens after you start moving towards it, you have to take the initiative and move forth. The situation won't improve all on its own.

Over and over, all throughout Scripture, God and his messengers encourage us not to be afraid of troubles. *"This is my command—be strong and courageous! Do not be afraid or discouraged. For the LORD your God is with you wherever you go."* (Joshua 1:9) Always remember that God is with you.

In the drowning waters that night of August 30, 2003, I literally experienced firsthand the depth of these verses. God was with me in those floodwaters that engulfed me. *"Do not be afraid, for I have ransomed you. I have called you by name; you are mine. When you go through deep waters, I will be with you. When you go through rivers of difficulty, you will not drown. When you walk through the fire of oppression, you will not be burned up; the flames will not consume you."* (Isaiah 43:1-2)

If you are going through deep waters, difficulties, and fires, don't stop! Keep moving. As I was taught, "Don't just go through it. Grow through it!" God wants you to grow from this hardship, to enrich your character, and to learn patient endurance in any situation. *"We can rejoice, too, when we run into problems and trials, for we know that they are good for us – they help us learn to endure."* (Romans 5:3) If you are willing to let God use you mightily, He will first always prepare you thoroughly. So, *Embrace It!*

As Joseph persevered in the jail cell, he didn't waste that precious decade. He grew in wisdom, favor, and knowledge of God and of administration. He went from the pit, to the prison, and up to the palace! When the time came, he was ultimately promoted to second in command over all of Egypt. God promises us a safe landing, but not always a smooth flight. Don't let the turbulence around you diminish the work of God inside you.

Try to imagine the impact to human history if this one man – Joseph – had grown bitter in prison and wasted his time, wallowing in his pity. *"Until the time came to fulfill his word, the LORD tested Joseph's character."* (Psalm 105:19) Joseph embraced that difficult time of testing with a good attitude and allowed God to develop him. He could have taken the easy road and complained indefinitely. The high road requires being *"thankful in all circumstances"* (1 Thessalonians 5:18), regardless of how unfair. Jesus, too, was wrongfully accused and betrayed by those closest to Him. Yet, He never complained. Instead, He embraced suffering, torture, and even death on a cross.

Rather than being a whiner, Joseph became a winner. Rather than gripe all through life about being a victim to his circumstances, he became a victor through God's sovereign Hand. *"Can anything ever separate us from Christ's love? Does it mean he no longer loves us if we have trouble or calamity, or are persecuted, or hungry, or destitute, or in danger, or threatened with death? No, despite all these things, overwhelming victory is ours through Christ, who loved us."* (Roman 8:35, 37)

Joseph let his circumstances become a victim to God's power. Rather than be sour towards God, he became more devoted to God. He magnified his God, not his problem. He refused to live by his situation, but started living by God's revelation. Follow Joseph's example. Don't tell God how big your problems are. Tell your problems how big God is!

Joseph's wisdom foresaw the coming seven years of shortage. He helped save Egypt as well as his own family, who moved to Egypt during the famine – setting the stage later for Moses and the Exodus back from Egypt.

In addition to the attitude you assume inwardly, the attitude you display outwardly can have a profound and lasting impact on countless others, often in unimaginable ways. They are watching to see how you respond. Some of my siblings remarked to me how they were influenced heavily by the way I peacefully and actively accepted our family's flash-flood tragedy. In part, they grieved in a pattern parallel to my grief. If I had gone off the deep end, perhaps they might have as well.

After the floodwaters engulfed my family, I embraced their lifeless bodies as I tearfully identified all five of them. Before the daunting journey to my awaiting hollow home near Kansas City, I requested to return to the flood site along the turnpike. I felt I had to face the flood and embrace its sting, firsthand and head-on. I took one step after another along the Kansas Turnpike towards the rescinded flood site at Jacob Creek to confront it directly. With my parents, pastor, and siblings at my side, I traversed the eroded embankment down towards the dreaded culvert, knelt at the creek's edge, and slipped my fingers into those muddy, sinister, now tranquil waters that had consumed my family and nearly drowned me. I felt I must embrace this moment in this manner so that it no longer had control over me. If I hadn't faced and embraced that place in person, it might have remained a vague, lingering menace, haunting my memories at any hour. I believed that if I could just see it up close and touch it in person, then perhaps I could better define it and defuse it.

As I touched the water, I immediately experienced a sensation that rippled through my body, then quickly dissipated. I felt as though God personally defused the sting in that sacred moment through these "holy" waters which had ushered my family Home and literally baptized me into new life. *"Death is swallowed up in victory. O death, where is your victory? O death, where is your sting?"* (1 Corinthians 15:54-55) A gush of relief and tears of grief flowed down my cheeks. I gathered five small limestone rocks from the riverbed to take with me, which I later cast into the Atlantic Ocean as an act of surrender.

In the hurting, I experienced healing by embracing it.

Later that same week, I actively and fully embraced every overwhelming emotion and element: entering my empty home, alone; choosing my family's five caskets; deciding on all the funeral arrangements; and immersing myself into the visitation, memorial service, and graveside burials. After the funeral, I chose and designed the gravesite headstones. I immediately began professional grief counseling, coupled with endless walks meandering through our neighborhood. I tried my best to make sense of it all and embraced every purging tear along the way.

At one point shortly after the funeral, a torrential rain began pouring at home. Again, I felt compelled to dive in head first. I stepped out into the rain, set my face like flint upward towards the rain clouds, and welcomed every cleansing, pelting raindrop that splashed onto my cheeks. The anguish was indescribable. Yet, the glimmers of healing were tangible and palpable.

I tried not to shy away from anything. I embraced everything necessary and worthwhile – particularly God's Healing Word – and immersed myself into sacred Scripture as never before. I even accepted the request to compose and deliver two press conferences to rooms full of cameras and microphones from local and national media. This task was completely out of my comfort zone. Yet, once I faced my worst fear – the death of my family – this assignment paled in comparison. God infused me with the grace and strength I needed at just the right time.

In hindsight, the words of hope I spoke at those press conferences were the beginning of ministry. After that, people and churches began inviting me to share at their Sunday service or Saturday morning pancake breakfast. Those first two years after the flash-flood, I offered our family's story well over 200 times. I embraced the agony required to relive the story again and again. The pain of my past intersected with the Cross of Christ to help bring healing. As I exhausted myself, I received the cleansing grace of God as He filled my empty heart with His healing virtue.

Likewise, Anna, a prophet who lived during Jesus' birth, had to face the death of her husband after only seven years of marriage. Many years later, at the age of 84, she still wasn't wallowing or wasting her wilderness time. Rather, she embraced it. *"She never left the Temple but stayed there day and night, worshiping God with fasting and prayer."* (Luke 2:37) Anna remains a consummate inspiration and example of how to handle grief. Give. Serve. Worship. Fast. *"Pray without ceasing."* (1 Thessalonians 5:17 NKJV)

Sometimes, to *Rise Above*, you must first press in and embrace the clouds you face – in order to climb higher and encounter God's grace. *"Then Moses disappeared into the cloud as he climbed higher up the mountain. He stayed on the mountain forty days and forty nights."* (Exodus 24:18)

Only God knows how long your difficult season of embracing may last. Moses remained in the clouds on the mountain for forty days. Joseph spent upwards of twelve years in prison. *"There is a time for everything, a season for every activity under heaven."* (Ecclesiastes 3:1)   Bask in that agonizing season. Don't try to cut it short. For *"God has made everything beautiful for its own time."* (Ecclesiastes 3:11) Yes, even the excruciating, embracing season can be beautiful, if you accept and experience it that way. For me, I've never felt closer to God than in the midst of excruciating pain. *"Moses entered into the deep darkness where God was."* (Exodus 20:21)   Don't shy away from the darkness. You just might encounter God there, as Moses did.

When King David was in the wilderness of Judah, he expressed his raw emotions, wailing, *"O God, you are my God; I earnestly search for you. My soul thirsts for you; my whole body longs for you in this parched and weary land where there is no water."* (Psalm 63:1) If you feel you're in a dry and barren wilderness with no relief in sight, cry out to God as David did. Search and thirst for Him alone. You will find that God will *"satisfy…more than the richest of foods."* (Psalm 63:5) Worship Him.   Sometimes the most intense adoration comes amidst the most intense anguish.

Amidst his difficult wilderness desert, David didn't just mope and moan. *"I lie awake thinking of you, meditating on you through the night. I think how much you have helped me; I sing for joy in the shadow of your protecting wings."* (Psalm 63:6-7) Rather than sulking, David began thanking and praising. Active gratitude helps shift our attitude, our perspective, and even our countenance.

During the years following my family's deaths, I cried out to God countless times. I desired Him more than food. I thirsted for Him more than drink. I did my best to thank Him and praise Him for all He had given me through my family's lives. Through thanksgiving, I found peace, rest, and shelter in the shadow of His wings, similar to King David's supreme example.

In 2009, my father was diagnosed with a cancerous lung tumor. I vividly recall our family's shock as we each individually faced the reality that "Dad has cancer." Worse yet, his life expectancy was three to six months at best. As a family, we collectively faced it, square in the eyes.

Thank God, my father led by example. We followed his lead. By the grace of God for over three years, Dad courageously gripped the pain and patiently gritted his teeth through every surgery and chemotherapy treatment. With my loving mother alongside him every step of the way, they heroically embraced this most challenging season of their marriage, with all its bumps and bruises, tears and fears, laughter and sorrow.

Throughout those precious yet painful 39 months, I repeatedly drove 200 miles each way from Indiana to Kentucky to tend to my parents. I sat with my father countless times in the cancer ward. There, he and nearly a dozen other patients around him permitted poison chemo into their veins to attempt to kill off those vicious, malignant cells, and hopefully prolong their lives.

My stalwart father fought so tenaciously that his physician ran out of available chemotherapy treatments. Apparently, my 82-year-young father had somehow managed to out-live most of the other lung cancer patients by a factor of two, many of whom were half his age! As my father grew feebler, I helped him navigate the restroom with his walker, IV, and all the complications they entailed.

After one especially exhausting day, I stayed awake all night with him in their bedroom. Dad and I took three hours to shuffle 12 feet from his chair to the restroom and back. He was half awake and half asleep. With one hand on his back and my other hand on his walker to help steady his movements, I prayed every inch of the way. As exhausted and depleted as I felt, it surely paled in comparison to my father's discomfort. That evening gifted me with the sweetest and most tender moments I've ever shared with my father. Sometimes the greatest trials bring forth the greatest treasures, if we have the courage to embrace them.

Dad valiantly and consistently displayed patient endurance like I've never seen, like I've never known, and like I can only hope to achieve someday. Indeed, my father never complained. Just ask my mother! The closest utterance I ever heard was when he graciously admitted once, "It's starting to get a little difficult."

Through my father's cancer ordeal, our extended family grew closer to God and to one another more than ever before. We each took turns visiting and caring for both our parents. During the occasional hours of overlap as we "passed the baton" from one departing family to another arriving family, we often shared precious minutes over the kitchen table, in between yawns, rubbing the sleep from our eyes, recharging the coffee and tea, or simply savoring a bowl of ice cream therapy together. As exhausting and excruciating as that wilderness season was, I wouldn't have traded these deepening familial bonds and memories for anything. I am ever thankful to God that we fully embraced it together.

I've never seen my parents more in love. They vividly transformed the worst of times into the best of times. They celebrated their sixtieth wedding anniversary in the summer of 2012. When my mother once asked my father why he kept fighting this cancer for so long, he lovingly replied, "Well, Puffy, I know that tomorrow morning when I wake up, I get to look at you." Now that's the kind of true love and remarkable marriage I'd love to obtain, especially after 60 years!

That November, nearly fifty of us crammed into my parent's simple townhouse to celebrate Thanksgiving. We truly gave thanks from the depths of our souls for every good and perfect gift from God. As well, we intentionally gave *"thanks in all circumstances."* (1 Thessalonians 5:18 NIV) This Scripture includes thanking God even amidst the pain of embracing the wilderness, perhaps even thanking the Lord *for* the pain. Yes, it hurts, but it also helps.

God graced us with a vintage holiday together. My father was in rare form, in good spirits, and armed with a hearty appetite! He feasted like a king. We all laughed, sang songs as I played the piano, and ate ourselves silly. True to tradition, I played George Gershwin's "Rhapsody in Blue" piano concerto, with my father close by my side, savoring every note and nuance. Occasionally when I perform Gershwin's Rhapsody, I flub a few notes here and there. I usually do my best to cover them and keep going. This time, however, the music seemed to roll off my fingertips flawlessly, even effortlessly. I felt as though I could feel both God's pleasure and my father's delight through my fingertips as they rhythmically danced across the keyboard. I sensed that God had especially anointed this moment as perhaps the last time I'd ever play it for Dad.

The next day, my father began coughing excessively. Alone I drove him to the hospital. He looked awful. They admitted him, and his health seemed to deteriorate exponentially thereafter. Within a few weeks, we requested hospice to help care for his final moments at home. During one precious exchange with just the two of us in his bedroom, I asked my father if he would lay his hands on my head and bless me. He placed his arthritis-ridden hands on my forehead and muttered, "God bless you, my son." That moment was simple and yet utterly profound. It meant the world to me. Two days after Christmas, on the day of my mother's birth, just four months after their sixtieth wedding anniversary, my father was born to eternal life. He breathed his final breath in his chair at home in their upstairs bedroom around four o'clock in the morning. Our hearts were half broken and half overjoyed for him. I helped provide the music for his funeral. As he had requested long ago, I played "Anchors Aweigh" as part of the recessional.

God exchanged the pain of my father's suffering with the joy of his complete healing in Heaven. Even after he died, he kept giving. He donated his body to science at the University of Cincinnati for medical students in training. At a memorial service some time later, the students referred to their donors as their "teachers" and "educators." From choices we make throughout our lifetime, God can indeed trade our ashes with His beauty. (Isaiah 61:3)

Don't waste your wilderness journey. Don't rush it or short-circuit it, either. Instead, *Embrace It.* Make the most of the present moment, even with all its challenges.

Chapter Four

Worship in the Wilderness

"Let my people go, so they can worship me in the wilderness." (Exodus 7:16)

The Israelites went into the wilderness to worship. Worship God there, even if it feels as barren as a desert with no one present but you and the Lord. Draw near to His heart. *"Draw close to God, and God will draw close to you."* (James 4:8) Offer up your tears to him as the woman did at Jesus' feet. Just as she held nothing back, but poured every ounce of expensive perfume upon Jesus, don't hold onto your loss or loved ones. Offer them up to God as your gift back to Him. Our loved ones came from Him. They belong to God. Don't try to cling to the past. Don't try to continually love your lost loved ones back as they were. Love them now as they are, where they are!

When she fully emptied and exhausted her perfume, this dear woman didn't stop there. She offered her tears to Jesus. Do the same. Don't hold back. Jesus was so taken by her gift that He called it a *"beautiful thing"* and declared that, *"wherever the gospel is preached throughout the world, what she has done will also be told, in memory of her."* (Mark 14:6, 9 NIV) God used her tribulation and sinful past for repentance and transformation. Your tears can be a *"beautiful thing"* when you embrace them and offer each one to God as your priceless gift. Like this woman's supreme sacrifice of costly ointment from the alabaster vessel, the fragrance of your precious tears offered in worship to God can change the atmosphere all around you. Similar to her deeds, your testimony may be retold for countless generations to come, impacting myriad people, helping them *Rise Above*. *"They overcame him by the blood of the Lamb and by the word of their testimony."* (Revelation 12:11 NIV)

In the desolate wasteland, God will gently embrace your heart as He did mine and whisper to you softly. *"I will lead her out into the desert and speak tenderly to her there."* (Hosea 2:14) Cut down the clutter and hear God's voice. *"My sheep recognize my voice."* (John 10:27) Let His Holy Spirit speak to you. Hear the *"voice shouting in the wilderness: 'Prepare a pathway for the Lord's coming!'"* (Matthew 3:3) Amidst your own barren wilderness, make room in your hurting heart for God. Prepare a pathway for Him to enter. *"Clear the way through the wilderness for the LORD! Make a straight highway through the wasteland for our God!"* (Isaiah 40:3) Don't rule Him out, shove Him out, or count Him out. Invite Him in. As you grip your pain, say Jesus' Name. Hear His voice. *"Listen to Him."* (Luke 9:35)

God made you. He loves you infinitely and understands every emotion you're experiencing. He will be gentle with you in the valley, through your healing process. *"But those who wait on the LORD will find new strength. They will fly high on wings like eagles. They will run and not grow weary. They will walk and not faint."* (Isaiah 40:31) Patiently wait on Him as you mend. Discover His power to renew your strength and restore your soul. (Psalm 23:3)

The key is to stay connected to God. Abide in Him. (John 15:4) Dwell in His shelter. (Psalm 91:1) Bask in His Presence. *"In Your presence is fullness of joy."* (Psalm 16:11 NKJV) Fix your eyes on Him, and *"think carefully about this Jesus."* (Hebrews 3:1) Worship and adore Jesus.

Everything hinges on your response and how you choose to embrace this agonizing moment.

Your hardship can either inhibit you or enable you.

You pain will either shape you or misshape you.

Your trial will either move your faith or prove your faith.

Much as an archer pulls an arrow backward and stretches the bow, God is drawing you backward and stretching your faith. From your perspective, seemingly caught in the middle, it makes no sense. You might feel as though you're moving in the wrong direction, backwards instead of forward. You might also feel that if God stretches you one more inch, you might snap! That's all right. Trust God. He knows what you can withstand. Keep in mind, too, that the further He retracts you, the further He can release you, when it is your time. For now, this pain is actually a good thing. *"So when we are weighed down with troubles, it is for your benefit."* (2 Corinthians 1:6)

While God stretches and retracts you, He also desires to aim you in the direction of your divine destiny. God aims you in adversity. Don't change His aim. Don't run towards addictions, substances, vices, or destructive internet websites. Don't handle adversity by clinging to sin, stupidity, or self-pity. Don't gravitate towards drugs, drunkenness, dysfunction, or promiscuity. None of that garbage will help one bit. *"Don't be drunk with wine, because that will ruin your life. Instead, be filled with the Holy Spirit."* (Ephesians 5:18)

Embrace Jesus. Only Christ can satisfy. Only the Lord *"restores my soul."* (Psalm 23:3 NIV) Gravitate towards God, *"safe beneath the shelter of your wings!"* (Psalm 61:4) Let Him *"hide you in the crevice of the rock and cover you with"* His mighty Hand. (Exodus 33:22)

At the foot of the cross, at the base of the mountain, we are transformed and transfused with the strength to carry our cross and climb that mountain. We discover that every stepping stone along the way – taken together and built upon one other with the mortar of faith

– forms a bridge that gives us the ability, tenacity, and propensity to cross the next crevasse that confronts us.

As I embraced my wilderness journey for many years, I did my best to follow these guidelines. I still do. Through it all, I've never done any drugs my entire life. I've never smoked, I don't need alcohol, and I steer clear of immorality and internet garbage. All of this is by the sheer grace of my sovereign Lord. I'm bragging solely on God! I want Him to be able to aim me and use me. *"If you keep yourself pure, you will be a utensil God can use for his purpose. Your life will be clean, and you will be ready for the Master to use you for every good work."* (2 Timothy 2:21)

I actively embraced three solid years of personal and professional grief therapy for PTSD. I highly recommend counseling to anyone who has lost a loved one, whether through death or divorce. I also ate lots of ice-cream and peanut-butter! I highly recommend that, too. Chocolate therapy is a very happy place for me.

Despite the difficulty, strive to keep your aim on Jesus. Lock your eyes on Him. *"I am focusing all my energies on this one thing."* (Philippians 3:13) What is that *"one thing"*? It is *"the prize for which God, through Christ Jesus, is calling us up to heaven."* (Philippians 3:14) So, set your face like flint on Him, knowing that He will not fail you. *"Because the Sovereign LORD helps me, I will not be disgraced. Therefore have I set my face like flint, and I know I will not be put to shame."* (Isaiah 50:7 NIV) Dig your heels in and boldly pray to God, "Lord, I'm

in it to win it." Be assured that God will not allow you to
be disgraced or put to shame. He has an even bigger
blessing in store for you.

Despite the circumstances and the typhoons of
troubles whirling around you, remain calm in the eye of the
calamity. Don't be distracted by what you can see. All of
that will eventually subside and one day pass away. Keep
your focus on what you can't see: eternity. *"So we fix our eyes
not on what is seen, but on what is unseen. For what is seen is
temporary, but what is unseen is eternal."* (2 Corinthians 4:18
NIV) This particular verse helped me tremendously after
my family died. Viewing your hardship from an eternal
perspective will make all the difference in how you react.
*"Since you have been raised to new life with Christ, set your sights on
the realities of heaven, where Christ sits in the place of honor at God's
right hand. Think about the things of heaven, not the things of earth."*
(Colossians 3:1-2)

So, how do you remain calm as you grip the pain
and embrace the hurricane? Much as Jesus did, asleep in
the back of the boat with His head on a pillow while the
fierce tempest pummeled the disciples. (Mark 4:38) He
embodied perfect peace. So can you. How? Don't let the
storm around you get inside of you. Trust God absolutely.
Abide in Jesus. Let Him dwell within you. Strive to detect
the Hand of God working in the midst of the storm.

Keep your thoughts fixed on His promises, as
Peter did when he first walked on water toward Jesus in the

middle of a storm. *"You will keep in perfect peace all who trust in you, whose thoughts are fixed on you!"* (Isaiah 26:3) Do that by reading His Holy Words – the Bible – every single day. As I was taught and often repeat, "No Bible – no breakfast; No Bible – no bed!"

Job modeled this impeccably. During his time of embracing every facet of pain and questions, he tried to find God somewhere in it all. *"I go east, but he is not there. I go west, but I cannot find him. I do not see him in the north, for he is hidden. I look to the south, but he is concealed."* (Job 23:8-9) He finally relented. Job surrendered to follow God's way, no matter what, even when it didn't add up. He ultimately trusted God to make sense of it all.

"But he knows the way that I take; when he has tested me, I will come forth as gold. My feet have closely followed his steps; I have kept to his way without turning aside. I have not departed from the commands of his lips; I have treasured the words of his mouth more than my daily bread." (Job 23:10-12 NIV)

Job treasured God's Word in his heart even more than food! He kept following God's way without turning aside. Rather than delve into addictive substances to drown his sorrows, he plunged into God's Word as his most vital nourishment. Follow Job's example. *"Put your hope in the LORD. Travel steadily along his path."* (Psalm 37:34) Don't fall off the bandwagon or drift off God's pathway. Actively place your hope in God alone.

If Job could do all this after losing his health, his business, and his whole family, then so can we by the powerful grace of Almighty God. *"As we know Jesus better, his divine power gives us everything we need for living a godly life."* (2 Peter 1:3) So, even when it's difficult to perceive God through your tears, stand on His Word. Dig in deeper, *"and after you have done everything, to stand. Stand firm then."* (Ephesians 6:13-14 NIV)

God can use your trial and tribulation for your transformation. Embrace the season of pain. Let God remake and reshape you. It can be a refining crucible of sanctification and purification to mold us more like Him. We can become *"holy"* as Jesus is *"holy."* (1 Peter 1:15)

Never waste your suffering. Don't let it be for nothing. Don't waste your pain or your tears. Let them count for something productive, fruitful, and lasting, perhaps even as a badge of honor. In the garden of Gethsemane, as Jesus fully embraced the cup of suffering and the cross before Him, He was able to bring salvation to all. *"While Jesus was here on earth, he offered prayers and pleadings, with a loud cry and tears, to the one who could rescue him from death."* (Hebrews 5:7) As Jesus did, cry out to God with your tears. Complete your suffering, allowing it to finish its work in you, to refine and ripen you. Then you will lack nothing and be ready for anything.

Never waste your wilderness journey. When you are brought to nothing, then God can do something with your life beyond anything you can possibly imagine, if you invite Him. Much like the dear woman with the shattered alabaster box, sometimes we have to allow God to crush us in order to exude the sweet fragrance inside. You may never know what God has planted within you until you let Him break you to release it.

Back in the Denver airport in the December 2006 blizzard, one hour turned into two hours, into twelve hours, and then twenty-four hours. No relief to the pummeling snow appeared, and cleared runways were nowhere in sight. People not only faced and accepted our mutual predicament, but many began to fully *Embrace It*. Some made their abode on top of luggage carousels, behind ticket counters, or in phone booths. Children ran races, played games, and watched movies. Athletic types put on their jogging clothes and exercised around the terminal. Winter enthusiasts broke out their snowboards and enjoyed the snow-covered embankments outside along the road. Business people were still busy with their buzzing mobile offices. The Red Cross somehow managed to bring in water and granola bars.

Thankfully as well, fast-food establishments, including Taco Bell and Panda Express, remained open as long as their food supply lasted. One thing I discovered for certain is that you realize how well you can embrace a situation when you and nearly 5000 all around you are on a steady, 24-hour diet of bean burritos and Kung Pao Chicken!

I became acquainted with new people, settled in, and used luggage and cardboard for a bed. We all made the best of it. A bad attitude wouldn't make it any better. At least we were all warm and safe. It could have been a lot worse. We had to intentionally *Embrace It.*

After Melissa and I faced and accepted Zachary's diagnosis of Down syndrome in 1997, we embraced our son and every element of his condition. I wasn't ashamed of him or his disability. I was proud of him and every hard-earned accomplishment, no matter how miniscule by the world's standards. Zachary wasn't a mistake. He was *"God's masterpiece"* (Ephesians 2:10) and workmanship. We learned as a family that God can use adversity as a means to grow closer to each another, closer to Jesus, and deeper in our faith. Even Zachary's disability became an opportunity to embrace this challenging cross and enrich our character.

We made countless trips to Children's Mercy Hospital for surgeries, therapies, and emergency room visits. We navigated Zachary's autism with his pediatrician and numerous therapists. We met frequently throughout the school year with his teachers and staff to continually formulate the best Individual Education Plan possible for Zachary. We attended monthly meetings with other parents at the Down Syndrome Guild of Kansas City. We helped raise funds through the annual Buddy Walk around Arrowhead Stadium. We learned sign language as a family to help communicate with Zachary and deal with his cleft palate speech challenge. We hired a behavioral therapist to help us learn to effectively discipline him, deal with his mood swings, and handle his thyroid imbalance symptoms. We enlisted the services of a professional disabilities advocate to ensure we fully received every possible program and service available for Zachary's benefit.

In short, we gave up our lives for our children. This is the purpose of parenthood, as we follow Christ's example. By embracing Zachary and his Down syndrome, we learned this essence of Christianity more deeply than ever before. We learned to put our faith into action and to let our faith graduate to trust. We could no longer maintain the façade of a cellophane faith. Our living faith had to be either vibrantly real, or nothing at all. We were finished with just "playing church" on Sundays. Jesus didn't save us just for Sundays. Trusting God means going out on a limb when you have nothing to hold onto but your faith. We learned this by embracing hardships.

"So be truly glad! There is wonderful joy ahead, even though it is necessary for you to endure many trials for a while." (1 Peter 1:6) Knowing that God has *"wonderful joy ahead"* while you embrace and *"endure many trials"* can help keep your attitude and eyes uplifted. This promise of God may seem impossible, and you may see no conceivable way that any

good could ever come, but rejoice and trust God through it anyway. *"I say it again—rejoice!"* (Philippians 4:4)

As you *Embrace It*, believe that God will ultimately redeem your suffering. He hears you and is near you. God desires to rescue you. *"The LORD hears his people when they call to him for help. He rescues them from all their troubles. The LORD is close to the brokenhearted; he rescues those whose spirits are crushed. The righteous person faces many troubles, but the LORD comes to the rescue each time."* (Psalm 34:17-19) At least three times in a row in this Psalm alone, God clearly declares His willingness and ability to rescue those who are crushed. The LORD declares in another Psalm, *"I will rescue those who love me. I will protect those who trust in my name. When they call on me, I will answer; I will be with them in trouble. I will rescue and honor them. I will reward them with a long life and give them my salvation."* (Psalm 91:14-16)

Long ago, three Jews named Shadrach, Meshach, and Abednego refused to worship the gold statue or serve the gods of King Nebuchadnezzar. The King was furious and gave them a death sentence into the fiery furnace. All three of them faced this punishment head-on with remarkable determination and strength from God, proclaiming, *"If we are thrown into the blazing furnace, the God whom we serve is able to save us. He will rescue us from your power, Your Majesty. But even if he doesn't, Your Majesty can be sure that we will never serve your gods or worship the gold statue you have set up."* (Daniel 3:17-18) Their response to the King's final offer infuriated him even more. *"He commanded that the furnace be heated seven times hotter than usual."* (Daniel 3:19) Not only did these three faithful and courageous Jews *Face It*, they fully embraced their fiery fate joyfully, as the soldiers *"tied them up and threw them into the furnace, fully clothed."* (Daniel 3:21) They didn't run or shy away. They realized that a time and a purpose exists for all things, including adversity and suffering, even to the point of death. *"And they did not love their lives so much that they were afraid to die."* (Revelation 12:11)

Some moments in life can feel as through God grabs you by the back of the head and forces your nose into the mucky misery, as if to say, *"Are you able to drink from the bitter cup of sorrow I am about to drink? Are you able to be baptized with the baptism of suffering I must be baptized with?"* (Mark 10:38) God wants us to *Embrace It* and deal with it. *"You will indeed drink from my cup and be baptized with my baptism."* (Mark 10:39)

Even Jesus' Blessed Mother, Mary, endured and embraced the unrelenting passion and death of her Son, our Lord. *"Near the cross of Jesus stood his mother."* (John 19:25 NIV) Mary courageously stood uprightly. She stayed. She looked death in the face and embraced it fully. She could have run or hid from the indescribable pain as she witnessed the Flesh of her very own flesh being crucified, and as she literally felt the prophecy fulfilled, *"And a sword will pierce your very soul."* (Luke 2:35)

Even when tremendous, overwhelming grief is involved, we can embrace the worst of situations with hope and joy for the future. The Bible assures us, *"Those who plant in tears will harvest with shouts of joy. They weep as they go to plant their seed, but they sing as they return with the harvest."* (Psalm 126:5-6) A harvest of joy is on its way, someday.

For now, don't simply sit in tears or wallow in pity. Don't remain parked in your past or stuck in your sorrow. Your situation won't improve by doing nothing. As one couple in Ohio answered when I asked them the secret of over 50 years of Godly marriage, "When you wake up, get up! When you get up, do something...worthwhile." As best you can, do something constructive, productive, and worthwhile as you embrace the hardship.

The one word that helped me heal the most since my family died in 2003 is this: *serve*. Yes, serve. It sounds backwards at first. When I'm in anguish, I feel as though I need others to pour into me. What I discovered is just the opposite. Turn it around. When you pour into others, then God will fill you. Make a concerted decision, even when your heart still aches, that *"as for me and my family, we will serve the LORD."* (Joshua 24:15)

Serve God by serving others. He will refresh and recharge you. *"The LORD will redeem those who serve him."* (Psalm 34:22) God will redeem your suffering as you serve Him. You will reap what you sow. In giving, you will receive. Give and it will come back to you. *"Your gift will return to you in full — pressed down, shaken together to make room for more, running over, and poured into your lap. The amount you give will determine the amount you get back."* (Luke 6:38) It remains one of the great paradoxes of Scripture. Yet, it's not unlike the process of exercising. By expending more energy, you actually come to have more strength. Similarly, by giving comfort to others, your soul will receive more comfort.

As you *Embrace It*, sow goodness amidst your tears. *"And don't forget to do good and to share with those in need."* (Hebrews 13:16) Keep your hands from remaining idle. *"Don't let evil conquer you, but conquer evil by doing good."* (Romans 12:21) Avoid evil temptations. *"Don't participate in wild parties and getting drunk, or in adultery and immoral living, or in fighting and jealousy. But let the Lord Jesus Christ take control of you, and don't think of ways to indulge your evil desires."* (Romans 13:13-14) Putting this into practice after my family died facilitated the healing process immensely. Keeping addictions out allowed God in. Staying clean allowed God's Comforter – the Holy Spirit – to restore my soul and heal my heart. As you remain pure, particularly during the challenging time of embracing the pain, you grant God permission to use your life for His purpose. Serving and fulfilling God's work for your life will shift your focus and heal your heart faster than anything else.

Do good. Serve others wholeheartedly. *"Turn away from evil and do good."* (Psalm 34:14) Minister to others.

Share your story with them. You might be surprised how it can impact and uplift the life of another struggling human being.

Take a small step and serve. One of the best ways I've found to mend is to turn my attention to others and help someone else in need. Shift your focus from inward to outward. Get your mind off yourself and consider others. Find someone who has been through a similar experience as you. Encourage someone with your witness. Uplift someone with your words. Cook some food and bless someone with physical nourishment. Share a brief moment with them. It doesn't have to take long or cost much. Volunteer at a hospital, retirement home, or food pantry. Give what you have to give. As God asked Moses, *"What do you have there in your hand?" "A shepherd's staff,"* he answered. (Exodus 4:2) God worked through Moses' staff time and again to perform mighty miracles. Use whatever is already in your hands. Out of your mess, let God bring forth a message and a ministry. Offer it to God. Share it with others. Watch Him work miracles.

Jesus emphatically proclaimed, *"For even I, the Son of Man, came here not to be served but to serve others, and to give my life."* (Matthew 20:28) We are to do no less. *"Jesus said, 'Yes, now go and do the same.'"* (Luke 10:37) The season of embracing suffering is the best time to serve others. Do it with a good attitude and a joyful heart. *"Serve the Lord with gladness."* (Psalm 100:2 NKJV)

I witnessed this principle firsthand as I shared my story hundreds of times soon after the flood. I poured out my heart and tears to others. As I emptied myself, God's Holy Spirit replenished me with refreshing gratification from those whose lives were deeply impacted. Speaking publicly in front of a room full of people was always my weakest spot. What I discovered is that in my weakness, God displays His strength. *"For when I am weak, then I am strong."* (2 Corinthians 12:10) It's not me. It's Him. It's not even about me. It's all about Jesus. *"This light and power that now shine within us – is held...in our weak bodies. So everyone can see that our glorious power is from God and is not our own."* (2 Corinthians 4:7)

I also profoundly experienced it on missionary trips to Russia, Haiti, and India, where I travelled after the 2004 tsunami to minister to those who had also lost their loved ones in turbulent waters, much like mine. As I gazed into the eyes of those who hurt, I saw their heart. It pierced my heart. It changed my life. It transformed me. It helped to heal my heart.

In the Bible, Ruth ministered immediately after her husband of ten years died. Rather than go her own way, she served her mother-in-law, Naomi, by traveling to her homeland and remaining by her side indefinitely. Despite her objections, *"Ruth insisted on staying with Naomi."* (Ruth 1:14) They travelled together and later arrived in Bethlehem during the barley harvest.

Rather than mope around in tears with her mother-in-law, Ruth got up and did something worthwhile. She didn't linger over her loss. She got to work. She took to sharecropping right away after her husband died. She worked the fields diligently, gathering leftover grain behind the harvesters. Even the foreman remarked, *"She has been hard at work ever since, except for a few minutes' rest over there in the shelter."* (Ruth 2:7) Her positive attitude caught people's attention. The field owner, Boaz, was so impressed by Ruth's kindness, service, and loyalty to her mother-in-law, that he showed her special favor and ultimately married her. King David was their great-grandson in the lineage of the promised Savior Jesus.

When you go out weeping, sow seeds of goodness and kindness from your tears. Turn your attention to others. Your witness and your tears are your seeds. Cast your seeds to the harvest. Cheerfully give part of your heart to others. You just might be amazed at the divine appointments that God arranges for you. Out of every great test can come a great testimony. Everything hinges on your attitude and your response.

So thank God and rejoice in your insurmountable difficulty. Through it God can develop your fortitude and endurance. *"Not only so, but we also rejoice in our sufferings, because we know that suffering produces perseverance; perseverance, character; and character, hope."* (Romans 5:3-4 NIV)

By the grace of God, I am able to still smile, not in spite of my hardships, but because of them. My outward joy is not a fake, happy-clappy disguise. Rather it overflows outwardly, precisely because of what I've allowed God to do inwardly. As I often pray, "Father, God, do within me what You must, so that You can do through me what you will." Allow God to work *in* your infirmity so that He can work *through* your infirmity.

As you probably well know, life is eventually going to compress you in some way. *"We are pressed on every side by troubles, but we are not crushed and broken. We are perplexed, but we don't give up and quit."* (2 Corinthians 4:8) Don't give up. Keep a bulldog grip on God's promises. Keep filling your life with His Word. Similar to a tube of toothpaste, when life squeezes you, whatever is on the inside is going to come oozing out for all to see. Pain reveals the stuff from which we are made. Resentment, pride, or anger may gush out when the pressure of a trial constricts us.

By God's grace, in 2003, when life had its worst grip around my chest, God's goodness and hope came pouring out of my mouth at both press conferences and afterwards. Thank God I had already filled my "tube of toothpaste" with years of hope, Scripture, and God's Word. *"What you say flows from what is in your heart."* (Luke 6:45) With what are you filling your vessel? When life squeezes you, what pours out? *Embrace It.* Embrace Him.

Step 3

Chapter Five

Past Your Past

"When darkness overtakes the godly, light will come bursting in."   (Psalm 112:4)

The night is usually darkest just before the dawn. As you embrace your hardship and grip the pain, don't give up, don't give out, and don't give in. You may feel as though the deep darkness enclosing you may never end. Yet, God has a great message for you! *"Weeping may last through the night, but joy comes with the morning."* (Psalm 30:5)

Good news! The dawn is coming. Good morning! God's mercies *"are new every morning."* (Lamentations 3:23 NIV) Our Lord is a God of second chances. He has another chance awaiting you. He's done it all through time, ever since Adam and Eve. He did it for Moses, Abraham, and King David. He can do it for you.

As with the flood of Noah, the rain didn't come to pelt incessantly or pour indefinitely. Rather, *"it came to pass."* (Genesis 8:6 NKJV) Everything has a season. This storm you're enduring won't persist forever. It didn't come to stay. It came to pass. Whether your predicament happened from something outside of your control, or perhaps from a personal choice you made, God still wants to give you a fresh start. *"We went through fire and flood, but you brought us to a place of great abundance."* (Psalm 66:12)

Your history does not have to determine your destiny. Your past is not responsible for dictating your future direction. It's not an excuse to blame for your behavior. God is the Author of your divine destiny. Get on track with His perfect will for you. It's time to get past your past. "Yesterday is not ours to recover, but tomorrow is ours to win or lose." (President Lyndon B. Johnson)

Don't allow the devil to deceive you with the supreme lie that you might never get past your past. Don't permit him to convince you otherwise. You can get through this hardship and you will. Surrender, release it to God, and let the past go right now. *"Give all your worries and cares to God, for he cares about you."* (1 Peter 5:7) Ask God to release you from the bondage of grief. Don't enable your grief to endlessly cripple your joy. As Jesus responded to the man who intended to follow Him, *"Anyone who puts a hand to the plow and then looks back is not fit for the Kingdom of God."* (Luke 9:62) Don't look back. Grip God's handles tenaciously and plow forward.

After all, some of what lies behind you are lies. Forget them! Get through your past. Let it go. Your past is not a barrier to God. Your past is only a barrier to you. Bitterness can be one of the greatest barriers between you and God. Choose not to be bitter, but to be better.

Don't react as Naomi did after her husband and two sons died. She wanted to change her very name and identity to bitterness. *"Don't call me Naomi,' she responded. 'Instead, call me Mara, for the Almighty has made life very bitter for me. I went away full, but the LORD has brought me home empty. Why call me Naomi when the LORD has caused me to suffer and the Almighty has sent such tragedy upon me?'"* (Ruth 1:20-21)

Certainly, you may never forget the past. Cherish those precious memories with grandparents, parents, children, and spouses. I'll never forget when Zachary once played by the pantry and dumped an entire jug of olive oil on the linoleum floor, then topped it with Cheerios. What a messy memory! Recollections, people, and hard-learned lessons from our past should especially never be forgotten. Learn the lessons and apply them. Don't repeat the same mistakes. Pain can be a fabulous teacher. However, don't use your past as an excuse not to forge ahead to the future, either. You don't have to be a product of your past.

The good news is that the magnitude of your problem is directly proportional to the magnitude of your solution. The bigger the pain of your past, then the bigger God's plan is for your future. I believe your best life is not behind you; it's still ahead of you. The size of your adversity indicates the size of your destiny. This hardship was not meant for your destruction. It was meant for your promotion. Even Abraham Lincoln faced and embraced the loss of eight elections before he finally became the sixteenth President of the United States. Just as God raised His only beloved and begotten Son from the dead, He can bring salvation from your situation. Redemption is what Jesus' resurrection from the grave is all about.

If you only gaze at the past you've lost, you'll never realize the future you've gained. So, turn around, behold and unfold the future God has in store. Step out in faith and embrace God's divine destiny for you. In the words of Oswald Chambers, "Leave the broken, irreversible past in God's hands, and step out into the invincible future with Him."

I realize it may still look bleak. I understand that no glimmer of light may be in sight. Nevertheless, believe it to be true. This, God can do, in even greater measure. Your latter years can be even greater than your former years. Your future can surpass your past.

As with the Temple of God, so it can be with you. *"The future glory of this Temple will be greater than its past glory, says the LORD Almighty. And in this place I will bring peace. I, the LORD Almighty, have spoken!"* (Haggai 2:9) Life is looking up! Your future glory can be even greater than your past. God can even instill within you immeasurable *"peace, which exceeds anything we can understand."* (Philippians 4:7) Let Him in. You may be in the storm, but don't let the storm dwell in you. Permit only God's perfect peace to reside within you to control your reaction.

Your painful detour is not a setback. Your setback is an opportunity for God to display His power. *"For since the world began, no ear has heard, and no eye has seen a God like you, who works for those who wait for him!"* (Isaiah 64:4) Let God work. Allow Him to show His stuff! *"Trust him, and he will help you."* (Psalm 37:5)

Take intentional time daily to be still in His Presence. *"Be still in the presence of the LORD, and wait patiently for him to act."* (Psalm 37:7) Turn off your electronic gadgets and hear His Voice. *"Be still, and know that I am God; I will be exalted among the nations, I will be exalted in the earth."* (Psalm 46:10 NIV) God will surely be glorified through this. Just watch what He will do.

3rd Step to Rise Above: *Replace It*.

Yes, *Replace It!* God has a marvelous, divine exchange program. He is the only God who can replace bad with good. *"So I will restore to you the years that the swarming locust has eaten."* (Joel 2:25 NKJV) God restores the lost.

Right now, ask God to trade your pain with praise, your despair with joy, and your ashes with beauty. He can and He will. He has done it in my life and He can do it in yours. *"To all who mourn...he will give a crown of beauty for ashes, a joyous blessing instead of mourning, festive praise instead of despair."* (Isaiah 61:3)

Don't give up now. As Jesus did on Calvary, fulfill the purpose of your pain by sharing the good with those in need. Jesus *"humbled himself in obedience to God and died a criminal's death on a cross. Therefore, God elevated him to the place of highest honor and gave him the name above all other names."* (Philippians 2:8-9) God the Father, Himself, replaced it for His Son. Through Jesus' death – the worst evil – He brought eternal life to us – the greatest good. Similarly, if you take a negative symbol (–) and add a vertical line to make a cross (+), you've just turned a negative into a positive. Similarly, when we take our negative experiences, problems, and regrets to the cross of Christ, He can turn them into the greatest possible positive. Replace your own calamity with something constructive, not destructive.

Pray boldly to God. Blend the passion of your pain with the power of His Word. As miserable as your past was, pray that God will return at least that much goodness to you. *"Give us gladness in proportion to our former misery! Replace the evil years with good."* (Psalm 90:15)

I realize that you can never replace what was lost nor your loved ones who died. No one can ever fill their shoes. Melissa, Makenah, Zachary, Nicholas, and Alenah can never be replaced. I still miss them. I still miss my father terribly since his death in 2012. However, God can replace the sadness of their absence with indescribable joy and fill the empty void in my heart.

God achieved this in ways I never could have imagined, comprehended, or even remotely manufactured on my own. *"You have turned my mourning into joyful dancing. You have taken away my clothes of mourning and clothed me with joy."* (Psalm 30:11)

Many years passed after the flood until my heart was ready to love and be loved again. I didn't try to short-circuit the gradual healing process during the long season of embracing the pain. I didn't recklessly jump into a relationship just for companionship or to avoid loneliness. I wasn't even looking. I was content that I had found true love once, been married for nearly 12 years, and been a father for over eight years. Now, I had to be content with God alone. I discovered that His Presence was enough. His grace was, indeed, sufficient. *"My grace is all you need. My power works best in weakness."* (2 Corinthians 12:9)

Then, through a divine encounter, I met, fell in complete love, and married a beautiful farm girl from Indiana named Inga. How she loves a man like me with a past like mine still baffles me. My heart burst with joy when she vowed, "I do" on that gloriously sunny, sacred Saturday in May 2006.

I thanked God beyond measure that I remained pure and obeyed Him during the excruciating years of embracing, so that I could give myself completely to my bride on our wedding day with a clear conscience and a clean heart. I thanked God for the strength and grace to love a woman again as my wife, knowing that occasional heartache and pain often accompany love along the way. A new relationship was a risk, no doubt, after the loss of my Heavenly family. Love often involves risk, pain, and possible rejection. Yet, I knew I couldn't stay paralyzed in my past by the fear of death. I could have taken the safer path and remained isolated and alone, safely cloistered for the rest of my life. I thank God that I jumped in and allowed my wounded heart to love again, so that He could *Replace It* with the joy of a new family. Inga was worth the wait. Love was worth the risk. I thanked God that she and I kept our marriage open to life, in whatever ways God had in store.

One year after our wedding, just when I thought my heart couldn't contain any more happiness, God graced us in July of 2007 with a mighty son named Ezekiel Thomas. The following year, we were blessed with a beautiful daughter named Estellah Eve in December of 2008.

In 2009, we endured the traumatic miscarriage of a little baby boy almost five months along and five inches long. My wife nearly died from all the blood she hemorrhaged. Inga and I faced the anguish of "little Dale's" death together as we held his deceased frail frame in our hands at the hospital ICU and buried him at a cemetery shortly thereafter. We embraced his brief life and every element of that shocking trauma. We implored God to somehow replace our mourning with gladness, for *"that time of darkness and despair will not go on forever."* (Isaiah 9:1)

Remarkably, our ever-faithful God answered our prayers the following year. In August of 2010, Inga birthed our strapping little man named Leo George. Astonishingly, eighteen months later, God graced us with another lovely daughter named Lola Elizabeth in March of 2012.

Who could have ever imagined, nine years after I faced and embraced the deaths of my precious wife, two mighty sons, and two lovely daughters, that God could somehow replace their ashes with the beauty of another gorgeous wife, two mighty sons, and two lovely daughters? How is that possible, but by the amazing grace of Almighty God? *"Great is his faithfulness; his mercies begin afresh each day."* (Lamentations 3:23)

God replaced my sadness with a new song in my heart. *"He lifted me out of the pit of despair, out of the mud and the mire. He set my feet on solid ground and steadied me as I walked along. He has given me a new song to sing, a hymn of praise to our God. Many will see what he has done and be amazed. They will put their trust in the LORD. Oh, the joys of those who trust the LORD."* (Psalm 40:2-4)

Trust God's Hand, and behold Him unfolding His plan. *"Taste and see that the LORD is good. Oh, the joys of those who trust in him!"* (Psalm 34:8)

As Shadrach, Meshach, and Abednego also remained faithful to God, even amidst the scorching flames of the fiery furnace, God remained faithful to them. God shielded them with such protection that *"…the fire had not touched them. Not a hair on their heads was singed, and their clothing was not scorched. They didn't even smell of smoke!"* (Daniel 3:27)

King Nebuchadnezzar was so impressed by God's miracle that he exclaimed, *"Praise to the God of Shadrach, Meshach, and Abednego!"* (Daniel 3:28) After these three courageous men faced their death sentence and embraced the fiery furnace, God replaced their destruction with promotion. *"Then the king promoted Shadrach, Meshach, and Abednego to even higher positions in the province of Babylon."* (Daniel 3:30)

Don't flinch when you face the fire. God wants to promote you higher. Don't run when you embrace its scorching heat. God will indeed replace your great pain with even greater gain and glory for Him. *"Dear friends, don't be surprised at the fiery trials you are going through, as if something strange were happening to you. Instead, be very glad – because these trials will make you partners with Christ in his suffering, and afterward you will have the wonderful joy of sharing his glory when it is displayed to all the world."* (1 Peter 4:12-13) God may very likely use the impact of your story to bring forth untold glory for Him around the world.

When Melissa and I raised our son, Zachary, we faced and embraced his Down syndrome fully. After two long years of gross-motor therapy (among numerous other therapy treatments), and with the help of a medical walker device, Zachary finally took his first steps on his own! After four lengthy years of speech therapy, eating therapy, oral-motor therapy, and sign-language instruction, Zachary finally learned to vocalize, "Da-da!" My heart leapt with joy at those two miraculous syllables. Zachary's path for nearly six years of his brief life was an incredibly arduous and painstaking one. Yet, I wouldn't trade him or our journey together for anything. Sometimes the most difficult pilgrimages are the richest. God replaced the endless tears and frustrations with even more laughter and jubilation along the way.

Let God be God. Allow Jesus Christ to handle the detours and disappointments of life. Ask Him to redeem even the past failures of others who perhaps abused, betrayed, neglected, or harmed you in some way. Don't harbor animosity or bitterness in your heart against your perpetrator. *Replace It* with forgiveness. *"Never pay back evil with more evil."* (Romans 12:17) Replace your past pain with the mercy of Jesus' Name.

Before Melissa and I married in 1991, she shared with me how her father had sexually abused her from childhood. Even though he repeatedly molested her since the age of eight, she courageously faced it. She found within herself the mercy to forgive him. Around age sixteen, through her unshakable determination to embrace that excruciating pain, they sought counseling together at a

Benedictine Abbey near Atchison, Kansas. Through the remainder of high-school and then during her years in Boston, Melissa and her father were still estranged.

Their healing process was very slow and grueling. All throughout our eleven years of marriage, Melissa had many vivid, dreadful childhood flashbacks. She would often curl up into a little ball, and shake and shiver. I couldn't even go near her until she was ready. I felt helpless, frustrated, and even betrayed by her father. His actions from long ago had violated our personal, intimate married life.

Melissa and I ultimately persevered together. After moving from Boston to Cincinnati to California and finally to Kansas City, God replaced that pain and bitterness with a beautifully thriving, renewed relationship with her father in Kansas. Forgiveness and reconciliation gave birth to beauty. He became a marvelous, jovial grandfather to our children. Living only ninety minutes away, Melissa often made his favorite tapioca pudding with melted chocolate chips stirred in. She still loved her father. She allowed God to replace that horrendous evil with remarkable good.

If you've been violated or abused since childhood, Jesus can replace your pounding pain and relentless, flashbacks by His mercy. Only Christ can heal and restore your wounded soul. He can heal your broken heart. Welcome Him in. Replace the pain of physical, emotional, or sexual abuse with the miracle of God's love and healing.

Let God replace who you *were* with who you *are* in Him. *"Therefore, if anyone is in Christ, he is a new creation; old things have passed away; behold, all things have become new."* (2 Corinthians 5:17 NKJV) Grant Him permission to use your tribulation for your transformation into a renewed person. *"Look, I am making everything new!"* (Revelation 21:5) Release the past and allow God to *Replace It* with newness. *"Forget the former things; do not dwell on the past. See, I am doing a new thing! Now it springs up; do you not perceive it? I am making a way in the desert and streams in the wasteland."* (Isaiah 43:18-19) God can water your barren wasteland and wilderness journey through the desert and bring forth life where once none existed. Place your full trust in *"God who brings the dead back to life and who creates new things out of nothing."* (Romans 4:17)

I recognize, particularly through Melissa's experience, that this leap of faith requires a great deal of trust, fortitude, and vulnerability. No one enjoys pain or change. We all naturally avoid it. As God stretches and renews you, it may involve a bit of discomfort. Let God change the way you perceive your past, your pain, your abuser, and *"let God transform you into a new person by changing the way you think."* (Romans 12:2)

As I learned, "If you don't like something, change it. If you can't change it, then change the way you think about it." (Mary Engelbreit) Adjust your thinking and let God renew your mind. Ask and allow Him to alter your thought patterns, *"for we have the mind of Christ."*

(1 Corinthians 2:16) You can do it through disciplined, daily prayer and by soaking yourself in the Word of God. Intentionally *"take captive every thought to make it obedient to Christ."* (2 Corinthians 10:5 NIV) As you spend time in Jesus' Presence, His Words will wash and refresh your mind, and purge your lingering memories.

Perhaps you keep pounding yourself with questions of should've, could've, or would've. I can identify. I asked these incessant questions to no end after the flash-flood. Perhaps your thoughtless words or careless actions caused extreme pain. Allow Christ to release you from your past failures. Replace them. Jesus can heal your memories and forgive your past if you accept His mercy. *"So now there is no condemnation for those who belong to Christ Jesus."* (Romans 8:1) Jesus does not condemn you. Neither should you. *"For God did not send his Son into the world to condemn the world, but to save the world through him."* (John 3:17 NIV) As Jesus said to the woman caught in adultery, *"Then neither do I condemn you."* (John 8:11 NIV)

Replace those relentless, pounding, persistent questions with the throbbing heartbeat of Jesus' love for you. If you've harmed or starved yourself as a cry for help, perhaps as the only way you thought you could purge your pain, Jesus can replace your endless drops of tears with mercy drops of His all-sufficient love.

Months before we married, Melissa deliberately cut her wrists one terrifying night. Maybe she was trying to release the painful memories of childhood sexual abuse. Perhaps her mind simply couldn't reconcile those horrific flashbacks of molestation with the thought of another man pledging to love her unconditionally for the rest of our lives together. Thank God she endured through that ordeal. God gradually replaced it all with inestimable joy throughout our marriage.

After Jesus' death, and His betrayer's subsequent suicide, the apostles must have undoubtedly felt tricked and traumatized by Judas. They had to face the pain of deception, then embrace every flood of unexpected emotion, and ultimately *Replace It* with Christ's peace and healing. They also had to choose a successor. *"So now we must choose a replacement for Judas."* (Acts 1:21)

Likewise, release the Judases in your life who have betrayed you. Replace the bitterness of them by first forgiving them. Release any grudges. Purge the wounds of all the venomous infection accumulated over time. Then replace the disgrace with grace. Ask God to redeem it all for the greater good. For, *"we know that God causes everything to work together for the good of those who love God and are called according to his purpose for them."* (Romans 8:28) *"Everything"* even includes hurts, betrayals, pain, regrets, missteps, slipups, and mishaps. God can replace and redeem each one. *"If you return to me, I will restore you so you can continue to serve me."* (Jeremiah 15:19) Return to the Lord. Let God restore you so you can be an effective and useful servant to Him.

Two of my seven siblings have undergone the painful difficulty of divorce. I've been told that it can feel like the death of a family, as your heart bleeds every day. Years later, I witnessed firsthand in their new and blended families how God can replace the trauma of divorce with the grace of healing and forgiveness. It's never easy by any means, *"but with God all things are possible."* (Matthew 19:26 NIV) Whatever your past pain involves, take it to the foot of the cross and let Jesus heal, transform, and *Replace It.*

Perhaps you are controlled by an addiction or feel trapped by a substance. Maybe you are looking for healing and answers in all the empty, unfulfilling places. *"Don't you realize that you become the slave of whatever you choose to obey?"* (Romans 6:16) If you feel captive to something other than God, ask Him to *"end your captivity and restore"* you. (Jeremiah 29:14) Pray, just as King David beseeched God, *"Don't let them control me."* (Psalm 19:13) Jesus can replace your desire for those vices with a yearning solely for Him, His Word, and His will.

Only Christ can satisfy the longings and cravings of your soul. Follow Job's lead. Amidst the loss of his family, health, and business, he still *"treasured* [God's] *words more than daily food."* (Job 23:12) Bask in Sacred Scriptures and allow them to *"penetrate deep into your heart, for they bring life to those who find them, and healing to their whole body."* (Proverbs 4:21-22)

I followed these instructions after the flash-flood, day by day, year upon year, as best as I was able. I literally felt healing virtue from God's Holy Word replace the death around me with life into my heart, health into my body, and restoration into my soul. Truly, His Word was nourishing food and sustenance to me. *"When I discovered your words, I devoured them. They are my joy and my heart's delight."* (Jeremiah 15:16)   As God replaced my ashes with indescribable beauty, it defied logic and human reason. It could only be the loving, surgical handiwork of Almighty God. Indeed, if God's Word *"hadn't sustained me with joy, I would have died in my misery. I will never forget your commandments, for by them you give me life."* (Psalm 119:92-93)

Let go of what lies behind you. Apostle Paul did. He even persecuted Christians and labelled himself *"the worst of"* all sinners. (1 Timothy 1:15)   Yet, he learned the key, to *"focus on this one thing: Forgetting the past and looking forward to what lies ahead, I press on to reach the end of the race and receive the heavenly prize for which God, through Christ Jesus, is calling us."* (Philippians 3:13-14)   He released his regretful past. Like a racehorse wearing blinders, Paul focused on eternity's finish line and lived for the eternal moment when God would replace every persecution, suffering, and sacrifice with *"the heavenly prize."*

In the years following the flash-flood, before I moved away from Kansas City and married Inga, I made many trips to the cemetery where my family is buried. I poured much thought into the design, construction, and placement of their red-granite headstones. The inscribed music and engraved scriptures are deeply meaningful. Memorial stones are Biblical, powerful, and necessary reminders. I've visited in the middle of the night, kneeling with tears streaming down my face. I've gone in the cold of winter, crying under a moonlit sky with a frigid breeze whipping against my cheeks. I've released colorful balloons from their graves on anniversaries and birthdays. Inga, Ezekiel, Estellah, Leo, Lola, and I even visited there together to reinforce our family's history with our children.

From my visits to the gravesite over the years, I've found that some people are never able to *go* to the cemetery. From overwhelming trepidation and white-knuckled moments, they simply can't bring themselves to *Face It* head-on. Conversely, other people never *leave* the cemetery. That beautiful memorial becomes a shrine, attempting to retain and hold their loved ones as they once were, rather than as they are now. Some people are so traumatized that they never replace yesterday's sadness with today's promise of joy.

I've learned that your past can either be a hitching post which you never leave, or a guidepost to help direct the remainder of your life. Pain can sometimes be like a Popsicle. We don't want to relinquish it, and often prefer to keep licking our own wounds, keeping them open and exposed. Ironically, consoling our own injuries can become so comfortable that we never heal enough to move onward. Comfort foods, attention from others, sympathy, and other healing balms can definitely help to mend the hurts along the way. However, taken out of balance and to extremes, they can also keep us trapped in our past and in a mindset of focusing inwardly, rather than outwardly.

I've heard it often said, "You are what you eat." You are a product of what you consume physically, spiritually, and mentally. That is, you become what you behold. Don't behold your painful past indefinitely. Behold God instead. Moses' *"face had become radiant because he had spoken to the LORD"* (Exodus 34:29), *"for his face shone with the glory of God."* (2 Corinthians 3:7)

Much as Moses did, you can radiate God's light and *"reflect the glory of the Lord. And the Lord — who is the Spirit — makes us more and more like him as we are changed into his glorious image."* (2 Corinthians 3:18) To do so, you have to spend quantity time with Him daily. Moses fasted and prayed for forty days in God's Presence on the mountain. From quantity time can come quality transformation.

Even if you're trudging through the valley, still bask in the glory of His Presence. It will transform your attitude and your very countenance. *"Those who look to him for help will be radiant with joy; no shadow of shame will darken their faces."* (Psalm 34:5) Gaze unto God for your source of help. In doing so, you will become more like Him.

Chapter Six

Sow What You'll Reap

"If you make the LORD your refuge, if you make the Most High your shelter, no evil will conquer you."
(Psalm 91:9-10)

I have found that if you are constantly identified solely by your trauma, people will begin to see you only that way. Some people seem as though they need to stay miserable just to be content. They appear to be drawn towards drama. At first, others may sympathize with you, but you may eventually repel them by continually wearing your hurts on your sleeve. Don't stay a squeaky wheel indefinitely. Like fueling a fire, spreading misery only breeds more misery. If you truly crave more complaining, discord, and bitterness, then just keep sowing it. It will boomerang back around and stick to you.

Instead, *Replace It.* Spreading hope exponentially breeds more hope. Like ripples in a pond, your faith-filled attitude can dramatically and positively impact more people beyond your range of influence than you ever imagined. "For it is in giving that we receive." (Saint Francis of Assisi)

If you need blessing, healing, or joy, then take the first step and sow it. Life is all about seedtime and harvest. You have to plant good seeds in order to reap a fruitful harvest. What I discovered from giving my life away is that the more you surrender and relinquish, the freer you become. Travel light on this planet. Heaven is our Home, not earth. Giving frees your heart from heaviness, your mind from worry, and your household from the weight of too much stuff. As I've heard it said, "Whatever you keep dies with you. Whatever you share lives on."

I witnessed my mother live this principle impeccably in the years following my father's death. She literally replaced the sadness of his absence with the joy of giving her life away. She still volunteers her efforts at church and retirement homes. She offers her time to her children, grandchildren, and great-grandchildren by visiting them around the country. She donates her treasure freely. She gives away paintings off her walls and articles from her home to the point where she barely has a bed on which to sleep! Astonishingly, my mother is free of the heaviness of grief. She is joyful beyond measure. She replaced it. Her countenance brims with bliss.

If you immerse yourself in the healing Presence of Jesus, you will reflect and radiate His glory and peace. You can become a source of comfort and healing to others, giving, instead of only receiving.

After the flash-flood, I served and answered the ongoing calls to share God's Good News through our family's story. Countless people mentioned how I seemed to have a sort of divine peace about me, particularly in my eyes and countenance. In no way was it contrived or natural. Indeed, it was supernatural. That peace can only come from God. *"I am leaving you with a gift – peace of mind and heart. And the peace I give is a gift the world cannot give. So don't be troubled or afraid."* (John 14:27) God's peace amidst your troubling storm will speak volumes to those around you and even help to comfort them.

Allow God in to replace your fear with His peace. Spend time at the foot of the Cross, adoring Jesus. Listen to Him. Worship Him. Read Sacred Scriptures daily and continually memorize it. Embed it into your heart, for *"the very words I have spoken to you are spirit and life."* (John 6:63) His Word will bring life to your body and soul.

"God blesses you who weep now, for in due time you will laugh." (Luke 6:21) When you've embraced the pain and planted the seeds of your tears in service to others, then God will replace those tears with a bountiful harvest of joy and even armloads of blessings. *"Those who plant in tears will harvest with shouts of joy."* (Psalm 126:5) In fact, the very element that caused your tears can be a source of blessing for others. *"When they walk through the Valley of Weeping, it*

will become a place of refreshing springs, where pools of blessing collect after the rains!" (Psalm 84:6) Your misery can become your ministry to others.

I beheld this firsthand as God birthed ministry from my calamity. After the literal rains and floodwaters, He brought pools of blessings repeatedly to help refresh people's lives, renew their faith, and heal their relationships. Within twelve years, I had freely shared my story nearly a thousand times to anyone who invited me, all without an agent, without charging fees, and by purely trusting God. I also began an orphanage foundation to help care for orphans and special-needs children worldwide. My initial vision was to fund five homes on five continents in honor of my five Heavenly family members. After the first eleven years, we had granted over $407,000 and helped fund seven orphanages in seven countries on five continents. Behold the Hand of Almighty God!

Perhaps you feel as though your agony may never end, or that God could never *Replace It* with goodness. Be encouraged. Without fail, the last trimester of my wife Inga's four pregnancies were the most excruciatingly painful. However, she knew the best was yet to come, even though it felt never-ending at times. *"That is why we never give up."* (2 Corinthians 4:16) Believe that God will give birth to a beautiful season of new life for you. *"For our present troubles are small and won't last very long. Yet they produce for us a glory that vastly outweighs them and will last forever!"* (2 Corinthians 4:17) God has such great glory in store for you that it will vastly outweigh all the troubles and trials along the way.

In 1996, about a year after Makenah's birth in California, Melissa nearly died from an undetected, ectopic pregnancy. Apparently, her tube ruptured and she collapsed on our bed at home. I rushed her to the hospital where they admitted her for emergency surgery and transfusion. Several years after that harrowing ordeal, we suffered yet another heart-wrenching miscarriage in Kansas City after our tenth anniversary. Through both grueling miscarriages, we faced death together as husband and wife. We embraced the unique waves of pain brought by each loss. After the second miscarriage, we searched our souls and felt drawn towards adoption. Eleven short months after a tearful, innocent informational meeting at an adoption agency, we flew from San Francisco to China aboard a Boeing 747 aircraft in January 2003 to adopt a special-needs orphan whom we named, Alenah WenYing. God replaced the agony and sadness of our two miscarriages with the joyful journey of love called adoption.

Back in the 2006 blizzard at the Denver airport, twenty-four hours slowly dragged into forty-eight grueling hours for all 5000 of us still stranded there. People grew increasingly restless, weary, and cranky. My wife, Inga, was by my side and about two months pregnant with our firstborn! She slept terribly uncomfortably the first night on the hard, tile airport floor. I managed to find a cot for her the second night, while I arranged our luggage side-by-side for my makeshift bed.

Finally, after being stranded fifty-two hours, we saw the light of day. They cleared the runways, and airplanes started lifting off the ground. We caught the first available flight anywhere east out of Denver. Inga's parents drove four hours to pick us up from Chicago-Midway, and we later retrieved our car, still parked at the Indianapolis airport. Together, we faced the blizzard and embraced all its repercussions. God ultimately replaced it with the joy of arriving safely home in time just before Christmas.

After the Israelites left Egypt, even though someone was hired to curse them, *"our God turned the curse into a blessing."* (Nehemiah 13:2) God reversed the curse. He turned it around. He replaced the intended harm with greater good.

Similarly, Joseph declared when he reconciled with his eleven brothers, *"As far as I am concerned, God turned into good what you meant for evil."* (Genesis 50:20) Joseph rose above. He didn't give up on God's promises. He held firm to God's Word. Joseph's forgiveness and God's goodness ultimately triumphed over evil, redeeming it all *"for good to accomplish what is now being done, the saving of many lives."* (Genesis 50:20 NIV)

God did it for them and throughout all of Scripture. He's done it for me. He can do it for you.

If your past is tarnished with regrets or sin that you feel God could never forgive, then repent and allow Christ to *Replace It*. *"Though your sins are like scarlet, I will make them as white as snow. Though they are red like crimson, I will make them as white as wool."* (Isaiah 1:18) God can redeem the worst. *"You will trample our sins under your feet and throw them into the depths of the ocean!"* (Micah 7:19) Replace the guilt with grace.

Perhaps you feel as though you'll never amount to anything. The opinions and judgment of others have beaten you down, stolen your fire, and squelched your dreams. Just as King David did, don't permit the low expectations of others to keep you from rising above them. Don't let others place a glass ceiling over you. *"People judge by outward appearance, but the LORD looks at the heart."* (1 Samuel 17:7) Keep your heart fully His, even if you are the youngest and smallest like David. After all, *"Human defiance only enhances your glory."* (Psalm 76:10) Adversity augments God's splendor. The very opposition you face is an opportunity to magnify God. Embrace the adversity – in whatever form it comes. Then watch God *Replace It* with His brilliance, as He did with David.

As a young boy, even David's father apparently didn't think highly of him. When Samuel came to anoint the next king, Jesse didn't even invite his youngest son, David, to be considered. After Samuel passed by all seven older brothers, he asked Jesse, *"Are these all the sons you have?"* *"There is still the youngest,"* Jesse replied. *"But he's out in the fields watching the sheep and goats.*" (1 Samuel 17:11)   Evidently, Jesse didn't think David had what it took, and relegated him to tend sheep.   Years later, just before David slewed Goliath, his oldest brother *"was angry.   What are you doing around here anyway?' he demanded.   What about those few sheep you're supposed to be taking care of?'"* (1 Samuel 17:28)   Yet, when Samuel first saw him as a boy, he knew David was to be the next king. *"And the Spirit of the LORD came powerfully upon David from that day on."* (1 Samuel 17:13)   Through humility and a heart for God, David rose above the low expectations of his family and became Israel's next king. God Himself called *"David, son of Jesse, a man after my own heart."* (Acts 13:22)

Much like David, God desires to fill you with His power so that you can *Rise Above.* *"Humble yourselves before the Lord, and he will lift you up in honor."* (James 4:10)   Doing so requires humility and submission to God's plan, to surrender control to Him and trust His powerful Hand of providence. *"So humble yourselves under the mighty power of God, and at the right time he will lift you up in honor."* (1 Peter 5:6) Trust God's timing to *Replace It*, as King David, Joseph, Job, and many others can affirm. The outcome may not be your way or your timing. However, if you embrace the difficulty with patient endurance and obedience to God, then the end result will be God's way, and it will be good. *"God's way is perfect."* (Psalm 18:30)

Eagles detect when a storm is forming.   Rather than steer clear of it, they *Face It* head-on to take advantage of its power. Eagles embrace the winds and thermals to propel them even higher. From the blasts of heat and bursts of energy, they *Rise Above* by leveraging the potentially negative energy with its positive benefits. They *Replace It.* Similarly, during takeoff, a pilot positions the aircraft directly into the wind to provide more lift, so it can rise higher. "Don't let your trials blow you down. Let them lift you up." (Woodrow Kroll)

In the same way, whenever you face adversity, adjust your outlook. *"I will climb up into my watchtower now and wait to see what the LORD will say to me."* (Habakkuk 2:1) Try changing your perspective on the situation. View it as an opportunity for God to lift you higher than you are personally capable. After all, *"He displays his power in the whirlwind and the storm."* (Nahum 1:3) God wants to raise you up from the storm on wings like eagles. Rather than ask, "What can I do to avoid this difficulty?" try asking, "How can I best handle the storm when it strikes? How can I improve from it?" We all have these choices. It takes resolve. It requires an irrevocable, absolute act of your will and determination to *Rise Above.*

After Job faced his dreadful loss and embraced every ounce of pain, he served his friends. He ministered. He prayed. Perhaps, he even forgave those three friends who had callously blamed him for the deaths of his family. *"When Job prayed for his friends, the LORD restored his fortunes."* (Job 42:10) God didn't restore Job until *after* he prayed and ministered to those friends who had hurt him the most. This powerful lesson should catch everyone's attention. Once Job rose above their offensive remarks and shifted his focus from inward to outward, then God replaced his horrid misery with double of everything. *"In fact, the LORD gave him twice as much as before!"* (Job 42:10) God blessed Job with double the livestock and even double the children. In addition to Job's seven sons and three daughters already in Heaven, God *"also gave Job seven more sons and three more daughters. In all the land no women were as lovely as the daughters of Job."* (Job 42:13, 15) What a consummate happy ending!

All through sacred Scripture, God replaces people's misery with double blessings. He did it for Job. He promised it through the prophet, Zechariah. *"Now I tell you that I will repay you twice over with blessing for all you have suffered."* (Zechariah 9:12 GNT) As well, God promised through Isaiah, *"Instead of shame and dishonor, you will enjoy a double share of honor. You will possess a double portion of prosperity in your land, and everlasting joy will be yours."* (Isaiah 61:7) Who couldn't use a double portion of everlasting joy?

What God promised for them, He also promises for you! *"Jesus Christ is the same yesterday, today, and forever."* (Hebrews 13:8)

Don't you love a good book or a good story with a happy ending? I do. God is still a God of happy endings! Heaven is the ultimate happy ending, when God will replace every drop of sadness with joy. *"He will lead them to springs of life-giving water. And God will wipe every tear from their eyes."* (Revelation 7:17) As well, the seasons and chapters in your life on this planet can have good endings, when you withstand trials with patient endurance as Job did, and *Rise Above*. *"Job is an example of a man who endured patiently. From his experience we see how the Lord's plan finally ended in good, for He is full of tenderness and mercy."* (James 5:11)

God is also a God of new beginnings. As much as Job suffered, and as much as he certainly loved the children he lost, his best days were still yet to come. *"So the LORD blessed Job in the second half of his life even more than in the beginning. Job lived 140 years after that, living to see four generations of his children and grandchildren. Then he died, an old man who had lived a long, full life."* (Job 42:12, 16-17)

In many ways, I feel a close connection with Job. I share a great deal of parallel experiences with him. Like Job, I still have a spring in my step. No one can steal my peace. I may have lost my family, but I didn't lose my joy. God is the source of my happiness. He is always good and *"His unfailing love continues forever."* (Psalm 100:5) I'm an ordinary man, but I serve an extraordinary God.

The flash-flood which caused the deaths of my family may have completely inundated me, but it didn't devastate me. It may have wounded me, but it didn't destroy me. Therefore, God can use it to make me stronger. *"The LORD loves us very much. So we haven't been completely destroyed. His loving concern never fails."* (Lamentations

3:22 NIrV) I know that God is not mad at me. He is mad about me.

You and I are still alive for a reason. God has a divine purpose for each of us. He has a plan for your life. He enables us to *Rise Above* precisely because we still have work to do. *"He has created us anew in Christ Jesus, so we can do the good things he planned for us long ago."* (Ephesians 2:10)

Let God refresh and re-create you anew. Whatever the issue you face, ask Him to *Replace It.* Step by step, day by day, you can move from being overwhelmed by life, to overcoming the worst that life catapults your way. *"Such people will not be overcome by evil circumstances. They do not fear bad news; they confidently trust the LORD to care for them."* (Psalm 112:6-7) I believe your best days are still ahead of you. You can be forever victorious in Christ's strength, if you choose to *Rise Above.* God has a mighty plan and purpose for your life. *"What is impossible for people is possible with God."* (Luke 18:27)

Jesus Christ established the ultimate standard on how to *Rise Above.* Death had no hold over Christ. *"God released him from the horrors of death and raised him back to life, for death could not keep him in its grip."* (Acts 2:24) If Jesus dwells within you, then death doesn't have to keep you in its grip. Christ abides within me, so death has no hold over me. *"And the same one who descended is the one who ascended higher than all the heavens, so that he might fill the entire universe with himself."*

(Ephesians 4:10) Ask Jesus to fill yourself with Himself, so that you can ascend and rise higher.

Many people aren't ready to live again because they aren't ready to die. Don't be afraid of death. Don't permit it to paralyze you. The fear of death doesn't have to hold you back. Jesus already died and broke *"the power of the devil, who had the power of death. Only in this way could he set free all who have lived their lives as slaves to the fear of dying."* (Hebrews 2:14-15) Don't live in fear. Live in faith. Dwell in Christ.

I was taught that FEAR stands for False Evidence Appearing Real. Fear is faith in reverse. So, replace your fear with faith. Don't gaze upon death and the past indefinitely. *Replace It. "I will put breath into you, and you will come to life."* (Ezekiel 37:6) Invite the waters of God's healing Holy Spirit to bring life to your own *"Dead Sea, for its waters will become fresh. Life will flourish wherever this water flows."* (Ezekiel 47:9) Your life can flourish and bring vitality to others.

Embed your eyes, your mind, and your thoughts firmly into God's Word, and *"look carefully into the perfect law that sets you free."* (James 1:25) Jesus will set you free to soar like an eagle, for *"if the Son sets you free, you are truly free."* (John 8:36) You have liberty to *Rise Above.*

Remember, *"The Spirit of God, who raised Jesus from the dead, lives in you. And just as God raised Christ Jesus from the dead, he will give life to your mortal bodies by this same Spirit living within you."* (Romans 8:11) The grace and power of Jesus is more than sufficient to raise your spirit off the ground today, and to *"raise* [you] *up at the last day."* (John 6:40)

You will get through this. *"The godly may trip seven times, but each time they will rise again."* (Proverbs 24:16) You will overcome this. *"For though I fall, I will rise again. Though I sit in darkness, the LORD will be my light."* (Micah 7:8) Miracles still happen. I see living proof every time I gaze at my precious wife and four children. I thank God for them and for His faithfulness to *"transform the Valley of Trouble into a gateway of hope."* (Hosea 2:15)

Come to God. He will heal, mend, and restore you. *"Come, let us return to the LORD. ...now he will bandage our wounds. In just a short time he will restore us, so that we may live in his presence."* (Hosea 6:1-2) God will provide you a safe, solid landing. *"So after you have suffered a little while, he will restore, support, and strengthen you, and he will place you on a firm foundation."* (1 Peter 5:10)

Out of your story, God can bring great glory. From your mess, God can bring forth a mighty message. You can choose to let God turn your mess into a miracle, your misery into ministry, and your test into a testimony. The choices are yours. You can choose death or life, curses or blessings, trials or triumph, tragedy or charity, mishaps or miracles, tribulation or transformation, whining or worshipping, adversity or advantage, disability or opportunity, pain or growth, mourning or gladness, complaining or rejoicing, griping and grumbling, or gratitude.

"I will turn their mourning into joy. I will comfort them and exchange their sorrow for rejoicing." (Jeremiah 31:13)

You can choose resentfulness that turns rancid or mourning that turns into dancing. You can flip what happens *to* me to what happens *within* me. You can choose to say, "Why me" or try instead, "Why not me?" You can choose to be pitiful or choose to be prayerful; to be sour or reflect the Savior. You can run to the TV or to the Almighty, run to the world or to the Word, run to the iPhone or to Thy Throne, run to Facebook or to the Good Book. You can choose to lose or win, to cower in pity or conquer through praise, to be resentful or be grateful, to wallow in self-pity or worship in His Presence, to be overwhelmed or to overcome, to remain stagnant in pain or rejoice in praise, to descend below or to *Rise Above*.

"And who can win this battle against the world? Only those who believe that Jesus is the Son of God." (1 John 5:5)

You choose.

"You have allowed me to suffer much hardship, but you will restore me to life again and lift me up from the depths of the earth. You will restore me to even greater honor and comfort me once again."
(Psalm 71:20-21)

"His children will be mighty in the land." Psalm 112

Mighty in the Land Ministry
Teaching Others to Live a Life of No Regrets

In response to ongoing invitations for Robert to tell his family's story, he founded *Mighty in the Land Ministry* to help others **Know God and Live a Life of No Regrets**. Robert still travels the world and freely shares his testimony through music, Scripture, and vivid visuals. (**No agent; no fees; pure God.**) To order his materials or to schedule a life-changing ministry event, contact him by phone at 260-515-5158 or at www.MightyInTheLand.com.

Mighty in the Land FOUNDATION
Dedicated to advance adoption and care for orphans and special-needs children worldwide

Robert has been led to do more than simply tell his story. In 2004, he established the *Mighty in the Land FOUNDATION* orphanage fund with the vision to sponsor at least five orphanages in five regions of the world to honor of his five heavenly family members. To date, seven orphanages have been funded: Russia (2006-Melissa Home), Rwanda (2008-Makenah Home), Uganda (2009-Nicholas Home), Beijing (2010-Alenah's Home), India (2012 –Zachary Village), Uganda (2013-Hope Village), and Haiti (2014 – Joy Village). A portion of this book's proceeds will help care for more orphans. For more information on the *Mighty in the Land FOUNDATION* visit www.MightyInTheLand.com or contact the Foundation directly for various 'non-cash' ways you can contribute:

Mighty in the Land Foundation
℅ National Christian Foundation
70 East 91st Street, Suite 101
Indianapolis, IN 46240
317-570-5850

Rise Above

Composed in 1995 in California, 8 years before the Kansas flash-flood.
Inspired by the Holy Spirit, Who knew I would need it.
Words & Music by Robert T. Rogers © 1995

When it seems like
Everybody's against you on the other side.
When it feels like
You've got no more friends left to help you fight.
That's when you've got to take a step back
And check your genealogy,
Because you come from a long line of kings and victories!

Rise above your situation,
Rise above your circumstance.
Stand firm on your foundation
And give the Lord a chance.

Rise above with wings as eagles
And soar the great expanse.
Greater is He within,
So, Rise Above!

In the midst of
Every evil device that the devil can find.
Overcome by
Every last attempt to try and stop your life.
You know he touched your last nerve
And you realize this means war.
But he's got another thing coming
Because you're in this with the Lord.

You're got to rise above every situation,
Every circumstance and every confrontation,
Because the Father, above, He's got a reputation
He'll get you out of your jam, and into a better situation.

Mighty in the Land Ministry

Fort Wayne, Indiana
260-515-5158
www.MightyInTheLand.com

Also by Robert Rogers:

Into the Deep: one man's story of how tragedy took his family but could not take his faith (Tyndale, 2007)

7 Steps to No Regrets: How to find peace of mind with God, others, and yourself (Mighty in the Land Ministry, 2013)

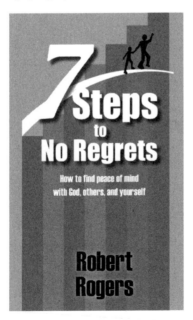